Vibrations of Manifestation

Heal Your Energy, Rewire Your Subconscious, and Finally Attract Abundance, Love, and Purpose

Codex Occulto

© Copyright 2025 by Codex Occulto - All rights reserved.

This publication provides accurate and reliable information on the subject matter discussed. It is sold with the understanding that the publisher is not offering legal, accounting, or professional services. For such advice, consult a qualified expert.

No part of this document may be copied, reproduced, stored, or shared—electronically or in print—without written permission from the publisher. All rights reserved.

The content is presented as-is, with no guarantees. The publisher assumes no responsibility for any loss, damage, or consequences resulting from the use or misuse of the information provided.

Trademarks mentioned are the property of their respective owners and are used for identification purposes only. This publication is not affiliated with them.

All copyrights remain with their respective authors unless held by the publisher.

ISBN: 979-8-89965-518-0

Imprint: Staten House

Staten House

Table of Contents

Introduction: No More Fluff, Let's Get Real	8
PART 1: The Frequency Foundation	**10**
Chapter 1: What Is Manifestation (Really)?	12
Busting the Myths	12
The Science Side (Without the Jargon)	12
What Works	13
Chapter 2: Vibes Don't Lie	14
The Energy You Are	14
Frequency Is Not Woo—It's Physics	15
So What Raises—or Lowers—Your Vibe?	15
Your Frequency Is Your Filter	16
What Are You Broadcasting?	17
Chapter 3: Desire, Intention, and Emotion	19
Intention: The Signal	20
When These Three Align, You're Magnetic	22
THOUGHT → EMOTION	24
EMOTION → BELIEF	25
BELIEF → ACTION	26
ACTION → RESULT	27
So How Do You Change the Loop?	28
Real-Life Loop Example	28
The Cycle Is Always Running. Use It Wisely.	29
PART 2: Tuning Your Inner Signal	**31**
Chapter 5: How to Raise Your Vibration Without Faking Positivity	33
Why Faking It Fails	33
The Truth: Your Vibe Can Rise Even on a Bad Day	34
So… What Raises Vibration?	35
High Vibe ≠ High Energy	37
Real Talk: Vibe Maintenance > Vibe Perfection	38
One Powerful Practice: The "State Shift Stack"	38
Chapter 6: From Doubt to Power	40
The Story You're Living	41
What's Your Core Story?	42

Doubt Isn't the Enemy—Denial Is	42
Neuro-Vibe-Hacking: Rewriting the Script	43
Action: The Reinforcer	44
Reminder: You Wrote the Old Story When You Were Powerless	45
Chapter 7: Emotional Calibration	47
Emotions Are Energy. Period.	47
What Happens When You Avoid Emotion?	47
The Emotional GPS System	48
The Feel-It Framework: Process Without Spiraling	48
Turning Emotion Into Momentum	49
What About Emotional Triggers?	49
Quick Practice: 3-Minute Energy Shift	50
Feeling Isn't Failure	50
Chapter 8: The Body Frequency Link	50
Your Body Is Your Broadcast Tower	51
1. Fuel: What You Eat Affects What You Emit	52
2. Breath: The Frequency Accelerator You Forgot	53
3. Movement: Motion = Manifestation	54
Bonus Frequency Factors	55
Your Body Isn't In the Way—It Is the Way	55
PART 3: Manifestation Mechanics	**57**
Chapter 9: Vision, Clarity, and the Power of Specificity	59
Most People Don't Know What They Want	59
Clarity = Confidence = Power	60
Vision Audit: Let's Get Clear	60
Specific ≠ Rigid	61
The "Why" Factor: Clarity with Depth	62
Visualization: Don't Just See It—Be It	62
Final Reminder: The Universe Matches Precision	63
Chapter 10: The Aligned Action Method	65
First, Let's Debunk a Myth	65
The 3 Filters of Aligned Action	66
Action Is Frequency Made Visible	66
The Ladder Method: Big Vision, Small Steps	66
When You're Not Sure What to Do	67

Aligned ≠ Always Comfortable	67
Alignment Isn't One-and-Done	68
The Universe Moves Through You	68
Chapter 11: Micro-Manifests: The 24-Hour Rule	70
What Is a Micro-Manifest?	70
Why 24 Hours?	71
How to Use the 24-Hour Rule	71
What If Nothing Happens?	71
The Compounding Effect	72
Add This to Your Daily Practice	72
Proof Fuels Power	72
Chapter 12: Quantum Timing	72
Linear Time vs. Quantum Time	73
Delay ≠ Denial	73
Three Reasons It Feels "Slow" (But Isn't)	74
Patience Isn't Passive	74
Collapse Time With Alignment	74
Practice: The "Already Here" Protocol	75
It's On Time, Even If It's Invisible	75
PART 4: Reality Design	**77**
Chapter 13: The Morning Frequency Formula	79
Why Morning Matters (Even If You Hate Mornings)	79
The 5 Elements of a High-Vibe Morning	80
The Mini Morning Formula (For Busy or Low-Energy Days)	82
Consistency > Perfection	82
Don't Just Wake Up. Turn On.	83
Chapter 14: Vibration Killers	84
Vibration Killer #1: Fear (Especially the Sneaky Kind)	84
When You Can't Avoid the Drain	86
Bonus Killers (That Sneak In Daily)	87
Vibe ≠ Isolation	87
Protect Your Signal Like It's Sacred (Because It Is)	88
Chapter 15: Using Environment as an Energetic Amplifier	89
Your Environment Is a Mirror	89
Create Anchor Points in Your Space	92

Redesign Without Overwhelm	92
Your Space Doesn't Have to Be Fancy—Just Intentional	93
Your Space Is Not Separate—It's Strategic	93
Chapter 16: Money, Love & Career	95
Manifesting Money: From Scarcity to Sovereign Flow	95
Manifesting Love: From Lack to Magnetic Alignment	97
Manifesting Career: From Struggle to Aligned Success	98
One Area at a Time, Full Focus	99
PART 5: Beyond the Wish List	**101**
Chapter 17: When the Universe Says "Not Yet"	103
The Truth About "Not Yet"	103
Why Delays Are Part of the Plan	104
3 Reasons You Might Be Hearing "Not Yet"	104
What to Do in the Waiting	105
What to Do When It Hurts	106
Quick Practice: Energetic Recovery Ritual	106
It's Yours—If You Stay Available to It	107
Chapter 18: Signs, Synchronicities & How to Read the Field	108
What Is a "Sign"?	108
What Is a Synchronicity?	109
How to Start Seeing More Signs	109
Common Signs & What They Might Mean	110
Red Light vs. Green Light	111
What If You Don't See Any Signs?	111
Final Practice: The Daily Field Check-In	112
The Universe Is Speaking—Are You Available?	112
Chapter 19: Vibrational Leadership	114
What Is Vibrational Leadership?	114
Why This Matters for Manifestation	115
The 3 Pillars of Vibrational Leadership	115
Who You Are Is the Strategy	116
The Magnetic Mirror Practice	116
Legacy Isn't What You Leave Behind—It's What You Carry Into Every Room	117
Your final formula for infinite becoming	117

The Manifestor's Creed	119
This Isn't the End. It's the Embodiment.	121

Introduction: No More Fluff, Let's Get Real

You've probably heard it before: "Just ask the Universe and you'll receive!" Or maybe: "Repeat this affirmation 111 times under a full moon and your soulmate will appear."

Yeah, no.

Look—if that worked, we'd all be billionaires sipping green juice in Bali. But most of us are out here hustling, overthinking, doubting ourselves, and wondering why that vision board hasn't shown up on our doorstep yet.

Here's the deal: **Manifestation isn't magic. It's alignment.**

It's not about "thinking happy thoughts" or pretending your life is perfect. It's about understanding the science and energy behind how your thoughts, emotions, and actions shape your reality—and then using that understanding like a GPS to create what you want.

This book is your anti-fluff field guide.

No unicorns (unless you like those). No incense rituals (unless they ground you). No law-of-attraction gatekeeping. Just grounded insight, tested tools, and a serious attitude toward energy, mindset, and doing the damn work.

You'll learn:

- Why your vibrational frequency is more important than your vision board?
- How to set intentions that stick.
- Why feeling your emotions is more powerful than faking positivity.
- How to take aligned action so the Universe knows you're not just daydreaming.

Whether you're trying to manifest more money, better relationships, a job you don't hate, or just peace of mind—this book will help you raise your inner frequency and get into the energy of receiving.

This isn't about "wishing." It's about **becoming**.

Let's begin.

PART 1: The Frequency Foundation

Chapter 1: What Is Manifestation (Really)?

Manifestation is not:
- A magical force that drops Teslas and twin flames in your lap if you think hard enough.
- A toxic bypass of real emotion.
- A spiritual popularity contest on social media.

Manifestation is: The process of aligning your thoughts, emotions, energy, and actions with a clear outcome—so that your internal world becomes a magnet for external experiences that match.

Think of it this way: your **reality is a mirror**, and manifestation is learning to shift the reflection by shifting what's behind the glass.

Busting the Myths

Myth #1: Just Think Positive

Nope. You can't positive-think your way out of a deep belief that you're unworthy. The subconscious doesn't care about your Pinterest quotes. It listens to your core vibration—your beliefs, emotions, habits, and patterns.

Myth #2: The Universe Rewards Good Behavior

This isn't karma points. You don't "earn" abundance by being nice. You manifest based on alignment, not morality. People with terrible attitudes sometimes manifest millions. Why? Because their energy is aligned with wealth, not their character.

Myth #3: You Must Surrender Everything

Surrender is great, but if you're using it as an excuse to avoid taking action or facing fear, it's not surrendered. It's procrastination dressed in spiritual robes.

The Science Side (Without the Jargon)

Let's ground this. Science tells us that everything is energy—including your thoughts, your body, your emotions. Your brain emits electrical signals. Your heart has a measurable electromagnetic field. Your body responds to your beliefs as if they were real.

Neuroplasticity means your brain can rewire itself based on repetitive thought and behavior. **Mirror neurons** show we're wired to tune in to energy (ever "feel" someone's mood before they say a word?). And **epigenetics** shows your environment—including your mental one—can influence which genes get turned on or off.
So yes, when you shift your mindset, reprogram your beliefs, and take aligned action, **you're literally changing your inner environment**—and the world around you shifts accordingly.
Not because the Universe is "rewarding" you.
But because your frequency—your energetic signature—is sending out a new signal. And reality, like a radio, starts to match the station you're broadcasting.

What Works
Here's what manifestation boils down to:
1. **Desire** – You want something. Not just kind of. You want it like your whole body lights up at the thought of it.
2. **Intention** – You declare it. You name it. You focus your energy on it.
3. **Emotion** – You feel it. You activate the emotional state of already having it, not just begging for it.
4. **Belief** – You clear the junk. The doubts, the inner scripts, the sabotage.
5. **Action** – You move. Consistently. Not frantically. But in ways that show you believe it's coming.
6. **Receiving** – You stay open. You detach from needing it now but stay aligned like it's inevitable.

This book is going to take you through every one of those steps—with clarity, tools, and none of the usual BS.
Because you don't need another motivational meme.
You need a method that works.

Chapter 2: Vibes Don't Lie

You've probably heard it before: "Everything is energy." It sounds vague, but it's a scientific fact. The entire universe—every thought, every object, every person—is made up of vibrating particles.

So let's get right to it:

Your vibe is not a mood. It's a frequency.

And that frequency is the language you use to communicate with the universe.

You're always manifesting, whether you realize it or not. The real question is:

What are you broadcasting?

And is it in tune with what you want to receive?

The Energy You Are

Your thoughts produce a **signal**.

Your emotions give **weight** and **charge** to that signal.

Your actions either **amplify** or **scramble** that signal.

Put all of that together, and you create your **vibrational frequency**—

Your energetic signature.

This signature acts like a tuning fork:

It attracts people, situations, opportunities, and experiences vibrating at the same level.

It also repels anything that's **not** in harmony with it.

Ever walked into a room and felt the tension before a single word was spoken?

That's not in your head.

That's **vibration**.

Ever met someone and felt instantly calm… or instantly off?

That's **energy talking** before words ever enter the room.

We all have an energetic field.

And it speaks **before** we do.

Always.

Frequency Is Not Woo—It's Physics

Let's nerd out for a minute.

Because this is where the "magic" meets the science.

Everything in the universe—everything—vibrates at a frequency.

The Earth has a measurable electromagnetic field.

So does your heart. So does your brain. So does your phone.

High-frequency states are associated with clarity, compassion, peace, joy, love, lightness, and expansion.

Low-frequency states are linked to fear, shame, resentment, stress, scarcity, and contraction.

Your **emotions**?

They're not just passing moods.

They're **data**.

They're **feedback**.

They are energetic indicators of what you're tuned into right now.

Gratitude. Joy. Empowerment. Purpose.

→ These emotions fuel your energy at higher frequencies.

Shame. Guilt. Anger. Chronic doubt.

→ These lower your baseline and muddy your signal.

This isn't about moral judgment—this is about **resonance**.

And the goal is not to avoid or suppress low vibes.

That's toxic positivity. That's spiritual bypassing. That's denial.

The goal is **awareness**.

To notice when your frequency is off-key, and then retune.

Like a guitar that went flat.

You don't throw it out.

You **adjust** it.

Same with your energy.

So What Raises—or Lowers—Your Vibe?

Let's break this down into practical, daily stuff.

Because your vibration isn't just about meditation and moon water. It's about what you do, feel, consume, and believe—**consistently**.

↑ **RAISES YOUR FREQUENCY**
- Taking aligned action (even if it's tiny)
- Expressing yourself creatively
- Honest emotional expression (no bottling)
- Gratitude that feels real
- Holding boundaries to protect your peace
- Speaking the truth—to yourself and others
- Breathwork, nature, silence, embodiment
- Laughing, dancing, crying, moving emotion **through**

↓ **LOWERS YOUR FREQUENCY**
- Chronic overthinking
- Obsessive comparison or people-pleasing
- Saying "yes" when your body screams "no"
- Suppressing anger, sadness, or grief
- Scarcity loops ("There's never enough / I'm behind / I can't do it")
- Consuming junk energy (doom-scrolling, gossip, fake connections)
- Disconnection from your body, needs, truth

This isn't about "fixing" yourself.

You're not broken.

You're a signal that sometimes needs retuning.

Get curious.

Not critical.

Start paying attention to what's **interfering with your clarity**—and gently clear it out.

Your Frequency Is Your Filter

Think of your vibe like a filter on a camera.

You and someone else could be looking at the **same situation**,
But if your frequency is clouded by fear or lack,
You'll see threats, rejection, and roadblocks.
If your frequency is aligned with trust and expansion,
You'll see opportunities, options, and momentum.
Same world.
Different lens.
High vibration doesn't mean you never have problems.
It means you become **resilient**.
You become **receptive**.
You stop chasing, forcing, overthinking, proving.
You start **receiving**.
You start **attracting**.
You start **responding** to life from power—not panic.
Because the universe doesn't speak English.
It speaks **vibration**.
When you become a clear, coherent signal—
not full of mixed messages and inner conflict—
You start to notice something remarkable:
Reality begins to respond differently to you.
People treat you differently.
Opportunities seem to "find" you.
You start hearing "yes" more often than "not yet."
And it's not magic.
It's alignment.

What Are You Broadcasting?

Let's bring this down to earth.
Right now, ask yourself:

- What's the dominant **feeling** I've been carrying this week?
- What **thoughts** have I been running on a loop?
- What **actions** have I been avoiding—or doing—that

shape my energy?
- Have I been in my body or stuck in my head?
- Am I leading with fear… or clarity?
- This isn't about shaming yourself.

It's about noticing.

Because awareness is how you reclaim your power.

Remember:

Your vibe is not fixed.

It's not your trauma.

It's not your bank account.

It's not your relationship status.

It's energy.

It can move.

It can shift.

And **you get to direct it.**

Every breath.

Every choice.

Every moment.

Chapter 3: Desire, Intention, and Emotion

Let's get one thing straight:
You don't manifest what you want.
You manifest what you're a match for.
You can want something with all your conscious mind, but if your energy—the total of your beliefs, emotions, nervous system, actions, and self-talk—isn't aligned with that outcome, you'll keep hitting invisible walls.
That's not failure.
That's feedback.
 It's the universe saying: "Get in frequency. Get in sync. Let your energy lead."
And becoming a true match for what you want?
That doesn't start with hustle or hustle culture.
It doesn't start with fake positivity or 27 sticky notes on your bathroom mirror.
It starts with the **Holy Trinity of Manifestation**:
Desire. Intention. Emotion.
These aren't just nice spiritual words. They're your power tools.
They're the three energetic dials that control your frequency.
Without them, your manifestation efforts fall flat. Like trying to cook without heat. Like launching a rocket with no navigation system. Like shouting into a canyon and wondering why nothing echoes back.
So let's break them down—**and build your magnetism from the inside out.**
Desire: The Spark
Let's be real: **Desire gets a bad rap.**
Somewhere along the way, we were told that wanting more was selfish. That craving success or wealth or joy meant we were greedy, ungrateful, or unrealistic. That it was somehow more "spiritual" to settle and be small.

That's nonsense.
Desire is sacred.
It's your soul nudging you toward your next level.
It's not about ego or entitlement—it's about your **evolution**.
Your desires are not random. They're **coded invitations**.
They're how the universe speaks to you and through you.
But here's the catch:
If your desire is vague, flat, or lukewarm—"It'd be nice if…"—the universe doesn't register it as urgent.
Desire must be alive. Clear. Hot. Focused.
This isn't about obsession. It's about energetic conviction.
Ask yourself:

- What am I craving at a **soul level**—not just what looks good on paper?
- What's the desire I keep **stuffing down** because it feels "too big" or "unrealistic"?
- If I could snap my fingers and receive one result in the next 30 days, what would it be?

Don't filter it.
Don't shrink it.
Don't "be reasonable."
Your desire doesn't need to make sense to anyone but you.
It just needs to be honest.
That's what gives it frequency.

Intention: The Signal
If the desire is the spark,
 Intention is the steering wheel.
It's the shift from:
"That'd be cool," to "I'm claiming this."
Intention is the energetic moment you go from wanting to **choosing**.
It's not a wish.
It's not a hope.

It's a decision. A declaration. A commitment that says:
"This is mine. I'm aligning with it. I'm moving toward it. I am no longer just thinking about it—I am becoming the version of me who lives it."
Think of it like this:

- **Desire:** "I want a fulfilling, flexible career."
- **Intention:** "I intend to align with work that supports my purpose, challenges my growth, and expands my freedom—and I'll take action on it starting today."

That's direction.
That's ownership.
That's a signal the universe can respond to.
Write this down (seriously—don't just think it):
"I intend to [insert your manifestation goal] by [timeframe, feeling, or milestone] in a way that aligns with my highest good and long-term growth."
Put it where you'll see it daily.
Revisit it. Speak it. Feel it.
This isn't superstition—it's **neurobiology**.
Your brain wires around repetition.
Your field calibrates to clarity.
And clarity is currency in the energetic world.

Emotion: The Fuel

Here's where it gets real.
You can have the desire.
You can write down the clearest intention in the world.
But if the **emotional signature** behind it is flat, anxious, fearful, or doubtful?
Your signal gets scrambled.
You short-circuit the magnetism.
Emotion is what powers the whole thing.
It's the energetic voltage behind your manifestation.

It's the frequency the universe picks up on.
Here's the paradox:
You don't manifest the thing.
You manifest the **feeling** you believe that thing will give you.
So reverse-engineer it.

- If you want money—what's the feeling you're after? Freedom? Expansion? Stability?
- If you want love—are you craving connection, safety, and belonging?
- If you want purpose—maybe you want impact, clarity, and meaning.

Now—here's the key:
Don't wait until the thing arrives to feel the feeling.
Feel it now.
You don't need to fake it. You need to activate it.
Try this:

- Visualize a moment where your desire is already real—vividly.
- Drop into the emotion—not just the mental image. Where does that feeling live in your body? What's the texture of it? The temperature?
- Breathe into it. Let it **soak into your nervous system.**
- Sit in that state for just 60 seconds a day.

That emotional imprint becomes your **frequency anchor.**
It tells the universe:
"This is who I am becoming. This is where I'm broadcasting from. Match me."

When These Three Align, You're Magnetic

Desire is the **match.**
Intention is the **flame.**
Emotion is the **fire.**

Together, they create a frequency that the universe can't ignore.
When you activate all three, you don't have to beg.
 You don't have to hustle.
 You don't have to micromanage every detail.
You just have to hold the signal—consistently enough that your **inner world becomes coherent.**
Because coherent energy bends reality.
 It bends time.
 It bends probability.
You don't need to be perfect.
 You just need to be **aligned often enough** that the energetic momentum takes over.
So the next time you feel off-track, stuck, or uncertain, don't spiral. Don't start over. Just check-in:
Have I connected to a **clear, bold, soul-level desire**?
Have I set a real **intention** that directs my choices?
Am I feeling **emotionally aligned** with the version of me that already lives this?
That's your recalibration point.
That's your power reset.
That's your signal return.
Because when those three forces converge?
You don't chase the dream.
You become the magnet.
And when you become the magnet, the universe moves.

Chapter 4: The Cycle of Manifestation

Let's stop pretending manifestation is some mystical secret locked away in ancient scrolls or vision boards.

It's not reserved for the lucky few.

It's not only for people who can sit in meditation for two hours a day.

It's not magic. It's a system. A pattern. A loop.

And once you understand the loop—really get it—you stop feeling like life is happening to you.

You realize it's happening to you. Through you. With you.

This isn't about spiritual theory.

It's about energetic cause and effect.

Here's the real manifestation engine:

THOUGHT → EMOTION → BELIEF → ACTION → RESULT → (loops back to) THOUGHT

This is the cycle that's shaping your reality every single day.

Most people are stuck in it unconsciously, replaying loops that keep them broken, stuck, or waiting.

But not you.

You're here to use the loop on purpose.

You're here to become the author of the cycle—not a character trapped in it.

Let's break it down.

THOUGHT → EMOTION

Every manifestation begins with a **thought**.

But not just any thought.

Not the one-off "Oh wouldn't it be nice…" that flashes through your head once.

What matters are the thoughts you revisit.

The ones you loop.

The inner monologue that plays beneath the surface.

Repetition is what makes a thought real to your subconscious.

Repetition is what gives it power.

So let's say you keep thinking:

- "I never catch a break."
- "Money always slips away."
- "No one sees me."

Those thoughts gather emotional weight.
They start to feel true—whether or not they are.
And that feeling is what the universe responds to.
On the flip side, when you loop thoughts like:
- "Something good is coming for me."
- "I trust myself to figure this out."
- "I'm allowed to want more."

You build a very different emotional foundation.

Thoughts spark the signal.
Emotions amplify it.

This is why you can't just "think positive" while feeling anxious, doubtful, or defeated—and expect things to change.
Your dominant emotional state tells the truth about your frequency.
Affirmations don't work unless they land.
And they don't land unless your nervous system can believe them.

EMOTION → BELIEF

Feel something often enough, and your brain creates a story to explain it.
That story becomes a **belief**.
That's how limiting beliefs form:
Not because you sat down and decided, "I think I'm unworthy."
But because you felt rejected.
You felt fear.
You felt dismissed, abandoned, overlooked—again and again.
Eventually, your brain said:
"This must be how the world works."
And it wired in a belief like:
- "People always leave."
- "I'm not good with money."

- "If I try, I'll fail."

But guess what?

That wiring is not final.

Because the opposite is true too.

When you regularly feel supported, capable, and confident, you birth empowering beliefs like:

- "I'm allowed to take up space."
- "Opportunities come when I act with clarity."
- "My voice matters."

Here's the game-changing insight:

You don't have to believe something yet to start feeling it.

But once you feel it enough—consistently, even for short bursts—belief will follow.

Emotion is the bridge.

And you can cross it from either side.

BELIEF → ACTION

You will always act according to what you believe—consciously or not.

Even if your goals are big, if your beliefs are small, your actions will shrink to fit them.

If you believe:

- "I'm not good with money," you'll avoid checking your bank account or setting goals.
- "I'm not lovable," you'll ghost people who get close or chase the unavailable.
- "I always mess things up," you'll subconsciously self-sabotage before momentum builds.
- But if you believe:
- "I'm capable of change," you'll lean into challenges.
- "People value what I offer," you'll show up fully.
- "I know how to figure things out," you'll take more

risks.

Beliefs don't just shape your mindset.
They shape your behavior.
And behavior is the bridge between your inner world and your outer results.
This is where the energy becomes visible.
Where intention becomes a movement.
Where potential becomes the pattern.

ACTION → RESULT
Now we're in motion.
Action is where your internal reality starts sculpting the physical one.
And every action either compounds toward expansion—or contracts toward avoidance.
Sometimes action creates results instantly.
You finally send that email—and someone replies.
You show up to the interview—and you're offered the job.
Other times, it's cumulative.
You go to the gym for 30 days, and on day 31, you feel the shift.
You post online for weeks, and suddenly a client DMs you.
But in every case, results are **a mirror** of what you've been thinking, feeling, and doing over time.
This is why manifestation is not just about dreaming—it's about patterning.
This is **energetic architecture.**
Your results are not random.
They're **reflections**.
And once the result arrives—what happens?
It circles right back to the beginning.
The result reinforces the original thought.
You say:

- "See? I knew I couldn't do it."

- Or: "Wow. That worked."

That's the loop restarting itself.

And if you don't consciously intervene, it just keeps repeating.

So How Do You Change the Loop?

Simple.

You start at the **entry point** you can influence most today.

That might be:
- A thought you keep repeating.
- A feeling you keep feeding.
- A belief that needs challenging.
- An action you've been avoiding.

For most people, it's easier to shift emotion or action first—because forcing belief when your body is screaming "NO" just leads to burnout.

You don't have to overhaul everything.

You just have to **intervene once**—and consistently—until momentum takes over.

Here's how:

✔ Take one bold action as if the belief were already true.

✔ Feel the emotion you want to experience, even if just for 60 seconds.

✔ Interrupt a negative thought loop and replace it with something neutral but powerful like:

"Something good is trying to find me."

Don't aim for perfection.

Aim for **interruption**.

Then repeat it. That's how you reprogram your loop.

Real-Life Loop Example

Let's say you want to manifest a new job.

Here's the old loop:
- Thought: "It's so hard to get hired."

- Emotion: Frustration, self-doubt.
- Belief: "I'm probably not qualified."
- Action: You procrastinate or send out rushed resumes.
- Result: Silence. Rejection. Nothing sticks.
- Loop thought: "See? I knew it."
- Now let's shift it:
- New Thought: "Something aligned is finding me."
- New Emotion: Calm, curiosity, grounded hope.
- New Belief: "I have value and something to offer."
- New Action: You polish your resume, reach out to people, and follow up with confidence.
- New Result: Encouraging feedback. A warm lead. Maybe even an interview.
- New Loop Thought: "This is happening."

It's not a massive overhaul.

It's a series of small shifts—layered, repeated, reinforced.

And over time, the new loop becomes your **default setting**.

The Cycle Is Always Running. Use It Wisely.

Once you see the loop, you can't unsee it.

It's always working—for you or against you.

You don't have to fix everything all at once.

You just have to interrupt the part that's keeping you stuck—

And feed the part that's trying to grow.

You are not a victim of your thoughts.

You are the engineer of your frequency.

So build the new loop.

Choose the thought.

Feel the shift.

Anchor the belief.

Take the step.

Let the result come—and repeat.
This is manifestation.
Not as magic—but as mastery.
Now go run the loop on purpose.
And let the universe match you.

PART 2: Tuning Your Inner Signal

Chapter 5: How to Raise Your Vibration Without Faking Positivity

Let's get one thing straight:
Raising your vibration is not about pretending everything is fine.
It's not about forcing joy.
It's not about smiling through tears.
It's not about posting "good vibes only" while your inner world feels like a slow collapse.
You don't have to slap a grin on pain.
You don't have to say "I'm abundant" when your rent's overdue, your heart feels heavy, and your nervous system is screaming for relief.
That's not high-vibe.
That's **emotional dishonesty**.
And your body can tell. Your nervous system can tell.
The universe can tell.
You can't fake energy.
You either resonate or you don't.
This chapter is not about pretending.
It's not about bypassing.
It's about **real tools to shift your frequency—without lying to yourself to get there.**
Let's stop spiritual posturing.
Let's talk about what works.

Why Faking It Fails
If you've ever tried to "just stay positive" while you were grieving, broke, exhausted, or confused...
You already know: that it doesn't last.
It doesn't land.
It doesn't change anything.
Why?

Because your energy isn't stupid.

Your body knows when your words don't match your truth.

And when your inner world and your outer expression are out of sync, you create resistance.

That resistance?

It doesn't raise your vibe.

It distorts it.

It creates an energetic tug-of-war—between the version of you trying to be "positive" and the part of you that feels unseen, unfelt, unheard.

That static creates a muddled signal.

You don't manifest from what you say.

You manifest from what you broadcast.

And fake positivity is like static on a radio.

No one can hear the signal through the noise.

This is why pep talks wear off.

This is why empty affirmations don't stick.

You can't layer good vibes over unprocessed truth and expect clarity.

Your vibe can't rise from denial.

It can only rise from alignment.

The Truth: Your Vibe Can Rise Even on a Bad Day

Here's what no one tells you:

You don't have to feel happy to be high-vibe.

You don't have to be in perfect alignment to attract something better.

You don't have to erase sadness, fear, or anger to raise your frequency.

Because raising your vibe doesn't mean staying cheerful.

It means staying **real**.

It means being **present**, **honest**, and **emotionally agile**.

You can cry and still be in integrity.

You can feel scared and still be in motion.

You can feel messy and still be magnetic.
Integrity is high-vibe.
Truth-telling is high-vibe.
Owning where you are is high-vibe.
That's what clears energetic static.
So… What Raises Vibration?
Let's skip the glitter and unicorn dust.
Let's talk about grounded, daily tools that shift your signal.
1. Radical Emotional Honesty
Start with the truth.
Not what you want to feel.
Not what sounds good.
But what's real for you right now?
Say it to yourself:

- "Right now, I feel numb."
- "I feel angry."
- "I feel overwhelmed, but I want to find a way forward."
- "I feel afraid, but I'm open to a shift."

You don't have to post it.
You don't have to share it with a coach or friend (unless you want to).
You just have to acknowledge it—, cleanly, and without shame.
You don't heal by ignoring pain.
You heal by moving through it.
Emotional honesty breaks the illusion that you're powerless.
It gives your nervous system a place to land.
It re-establishes internal coherence—which is essential for energetic clarity.

2. Micro-Movements = Energy Shifts
You don't need a week-long retreat to shift your vibe.
You don't need a 90-minute yoga class or a silent forest.

What you need is **movement**—any movement.

Energy doesn't like stagnation.

And when you feel stuck emotionally, you're often stuck physically too.

So shift something, anything:

- Stretch your spine for 5 minutes.
- Take 90 seconds of deep, conscious breathing.
- Wash your hands mindfully and feel the water reset you.
- Drink a full glass of water while standing in the sunlight.
- Clean out one drawer or corner of your space.
- Put on a song and let your body move for the length of the track.

These small shifts are **pattern interrupters**.

They say to your body: "We're not frozen. We're moving again."

That's enough to begin a vibrational reset.

3. Lower the Bar (Strategically)

You don't have to "crush it" today.

You don't have to finish the whole book, run the marathon, or change your entire identity.

You just have to take one step that aligns with your future self. Lower the bar. Gently.

- Can't meditate for 20 minutes? Try 2.
- Can't face the full to-do list? Pick one item and finish it fully.
- Don't feel worthy of love? Text one person who makes you feel seen.
- Does the big goal feel overwhelming? Shrink it to the next move, and do that.

Tiny aligned actions send massive vibrational signals.

They create **proof** for your nervous system that change is possible.
And when your body feels safe, your energy expands.

4. Feel, Then Flip

Once you've named the feeling and sat with it honestly,
You get to shift it—with love, not with pressure.
This is not bypassing.

This is **emotional alchemy**.

Try this prompt:
"What do I need right now to feel 1% more grounded, safe, open, or hopeful?"
Not 100% better.
Not perfect.
Just one percent more resourced.
Then give yourself that thing.
Not a life overhaul—just a vibrational nudge.
You'll be amazed at what happens when you start stacking those 1% shifts.

High Vibe ≠ High Energy

Let's kill this myth:
A high vibration is **not** about being loud, bubbly, excited, or always "on."
You can be high-vibe while sitting quietly.
While resting.
While grieving.
High vibration is not about volume.
It's about **clarity**.
Some of the most magnetic people on the planet are soft-spoken, grounded, and even slow in their speech or movement.
But their energy?
It's clean. It's focused. It's coherent.
You can feel their presence before they speak.
That's alignment.

And it's available to you, no matter your mood, personality, or pace. Stop trying to perform your vibration.

Start embodying it.

Feel it from the inside out.

Real Talk: Vibe Maintenance > Vibe Perfection

You will not always feel high-vibe.

You're not supposed to.

You're human.

You'll have moments of doubt.

Grief. Confusion. Anger. Tiredness.

And that's okay.

The goal is not perfection.

The goal is recovery.

How quickly can you return to the center—not forcefully, but compassionately?

How practiced are you in not staying stuck?

That's the real magic.

Every time you notice a misalignment and return to coherence,

You're building resilience.

You're training your field.

You're creating a life that reflects your new baseline.

That practice is the manifestation.

Not the perfect state.

The return to self.

One Powerful Practice: The "State Shift Stack"

Use this when your energy is scrambled and you need a fast reset.

You don't need anything fancy—just presence.

1. **Name It**
   → What am I feeling right now? (Use real, raw words: tired, jealous, numb, furious...)
2. **Normalize It**
   → This is okay. This is part of being human. I don't need to

judge it.

3. **Move It**

→ What can I do to move this energy physically? (Walk, shake, dance, cry, breathe.)

4. **Nourish It**

→ What support do I need right now—emotionally, physically, or spiritually?

5. **Next Step**

→ What's one small aligned action I can take from this state? Not after I feel better—but now.

Repeat this whenever you feel off-track.

It takes five minutes. Sometimes less.

And it works.

Chapter 6: From Doubt to Power

Let's talk about the voice in your head.
You know the one.
The quiet commentator that shows up right before you're about to do something new.
The one that whispers behind your goals, your decisions, your "maybe I can…"
It says things like:
"You're not ready yet."
"It's probably too late for you."
"Who do you think you are?"
"Don't get your hopes up."
Sometimes it's harsh.
Sometimes it's subtle—just a small tug of hesitation or a flicker of fear.
But let's get something straight:
That voice isn't the real problem.
Believing it is.
Because here's what's real:
You don't manifest what you want.
You manifest what your **nervous system** believes is **safe, familiar,** or at least **possible.**
So if your inner story is running on a loop of doubt, guilt, fear, scarcity, or unworthiness…
It won't matter how many affirmations you write or vision boards you glue together.
Your frequency will short-circuit every time you get close to what you say you want.
But here's the truth that sets you free:
You don't have to fight the old story.
You just have to **rewrite** it.

Not through denial.

Not through pretending.

But through realignment—emotionally, mentally, energetically, and physically.

Let's break it down.

The Story You're Living

Every single person is living a story.

Not the one we tell at dinner parties.

Not the one we post on Instagram.

But the unspoken one.

The one we broadcast with our energy, our choices, our reactions, and our patterns.

And here's the thing most people never question:

Most of that story was written before you had a say in it.

Let's name a few of the authors:

- Childhood conditioning
- Cultural rules and expectations
- Generational trauma
- Fear-based systems (school, religion, media)
- Personal experiences interpreted through pain

You were **programmed**.

Not because you're broken—because you were human.

And young. And impressionable.

That wasn't your fault.

But here's the kicker:

Staying stuck in a script you didn't choose?

That's on you now.

Because whether you realize it or not:

The story in your head = the vibration you're sending out.

If your inner narrative says:

- "I'm too late."
- "Things never work out for me."

- "Love always ends in pain."
- "Money is hard to earn."
- "People can't be trusted."

Then that's what your frequency is tuned to.

And the universe responds to **your energy**, not your wish list.

What's Your Core Story?

Let's make this real.

Grab a journal—or open your notes app—and complete these prompts, fast and unfiltered:

- Money is...
- Love is...
- I always...
- People usually...
- My life tends to...
- I'm not the kind of person who...

Now pause.

Look at what just came out.

Read those back slowly.

That's your **vibrational script**.

That's the subconscious story shaping your outer world.

And here's the good news:

This is not about shame.

It's not about beating yourself up.

It's about finally seeing the pattern.

Because you can't shift what you're afraid to name.

Awareness is the first act of energetic rebellion.

So don't judge it.

Study it.

Then prepare to rewrite it.

Doubt Isn't the Enemy—Denial Is

Let's debunk another myth:

You don't have to be **fearless** to manifest.

You don't need to "have it all figured out."
What you do need is **awareness**.
Doubt doesn't destroy manifestation.
Unconscious doubt does.
The kind you suppress.
The kind you ignore.
The kind that steers your choices from the backseat.
Doubt is not the villain.
It's a signal:
"You're bumping into an outdated belief."
What kills your vibe isn't the presence of doubt.
It's pretending it's not there.
Or worse—letting it silently run the show.
Your job isn't to never hear the voice.
Your job is to say:
"Hey, I hear you. I know you're trying to protect me. But you don't get to make the decisions anymore."
That's how you start **dis-identifying** with your old narrative.
You stop reacting to it as if it's the truth.
You start recognizing it as a well-worn pattern—and nothing more.

Neuro-Vibe-Hacking: Rewriting the Script

Let's talk **brain** meets **energy**.
Every thought you think creates a tiny electrical signal.
Repeat that thought enough, especially with emotional intensity, and you carve a neural pathway.
Do it for years? That pathway becomes a **superhighway**—your default.
But here's the exciting part:
Your brain doesn't know the difference between real experience and vivid imagination.
That means when you intentionally visualize a new outcome—and **feel** it in your body—you start to rewire your internal GPS.

You fire new neurons.

You shift the emotional blueprint.

You raise your energetic frequency.

Want to try?

Daily 3-Minute Practice:

1. **Pick a new belief** (e.g., "I am supported," "My voice matters," "Abundance flows to me.")
2. **Close your eyes.** Imagine a scene where this belief is already true. Use color, sound, and motion.
3. **Feel it.** Where in your body would this version of you feel activated? Calm? Confident? Safe?
4. **Anchor it.** Breathe in while holding the image. Exhale while repeating the belief silently.
5. **Repeat daily** for 21 days. You're not "just visualizing"—you're **reprogramming your signal**.

This is how you stop reciting affirmations—and start embodying them.

Action: The Reinforcer

You can journal all day.

You can meditate on your worthiness until you float.

But nothing locks in a new identity-like **action**.

Belief follows behavior.

So here's the deal:

Every time you act like the new story is already true, you make it easier to believe.

You make it safer for your nervous system to accept.

You create momentum.

Not fake confidence.

Just real decisions from a new energetic baseline.

Try this:

- Want to believe you're abundant? Pay your bills with intention—not dread.

- Want to believe you're worthy? Stop chasing people who treat you like a backup plan.
- Want to believe you're creative? Publish the post. Share the idea. Start before you're ready.

Every small, aligned action is a **vote** for your new identity.

It tells the universe: "I'm serious."

It tells your body: "We're safe here."

And repeated votes become a new default.

Reminder: You Wrote the Old Story When You Were Powerless But You're Not Powerless Anymore

You are not that five-year-old who thought love had to be earned.

You are not that teenager who learned to disappear to avoid judgment.

You are not the younger version of you who equated struggle with safety or success.

You are here.

Reading this.

I awake enough to question the script.

That means the pen is back in your hand.

You don't have to change the entire novel in one day.

Just one page.

One line.

One belief.

One choice.

Write a story that holds you.

One that's honest, bold, and rooted in possibility.

Because your new story doesn't need to be perfect.

It just needs to be **yours**.

Are you ready?

Pick up the pen.

Let's rewrite the signal.

One truth at a time.

Chapter 7: Emotional Calibration

Here's the unpopular truth:
Your emotions are not a problem.
They're not getting in the way of your manifestation—they are the way.
If you're trying to force "good vibes only" while shoving down real feelings, you're not raising your frequency. You're suppressing your signal.
And a suppressed signal is full of static.
In this chapter, we'll explore how to **feel your emotions fully, channel them intentionally**, and stop letting them hijack or stall your manifestation power.

Emotions Are Energy. Period.
Let's bring it back to basics:
The word emotion means **energy in motion.**
That means emotions aren't just mental—they're physical, vibrational currents moving through your body. If you block them, they stagnate. If you ignore them, they sneak into your decisions.
But when you feel them with awareness?
You transmute them. You use them. They become fuel.

What Happens When You Avoid Emotion?
Quick answer:
You start manifesting from resistance, not alignment.
Examples:
- You suppress grief → you manifest tension, confusion, isolation.
- You avoid anger → you manifest resentment and energetic leaks.
- You bypass fear → you manifest chaos, self-sabotage, or half-hearted effort.

In other words:

What you won't feel, you can't fully heal—or transform.

But you don't need to spiral into your emotions to move through them.

You just need to stop being afraid of them.

The Emotional GPS System

Every emotion has a purpose. Here's a simple way to decode them:

Emotion	Message	Frequency Tendency
Joy / Gratitude	You're aligned. Keep going.	High
Desire / Longing	You're expanding. Lean in.	High-ish
Fear	There's the risk—check alignment.	Mid-low
Anger	A boundary has been crossed.	Variable
Sadness	Something wants to be released.	Mid
Shame / Guilt	You're holding a distorted self-image.	Low
Apathy / Numbness	You've disconnected from the energy flow.	Lowest

None of these emotions are "bad."

But some help you manifest faster. Others slow you down—not because they're wrong, but because they need attention before you can move freely.

The Feel-It Framework: Process Without Spiraling

Here's a simple 5-step method to calibrate any emotion:

1. Name It

Avoid vague terms like "bad" or "off." Get specific.

→ "I feel angry." "I feel anxious." "I feel sad and stuck."

2. Locate It

Where is it in your body?

Tension in the jaw? Flutter in the gut? Heat in the chest?
This pulls you out of mental looping and into somatic awareness—where real healing starts.

3. Breathe Through It

No fixing. Just be with it. Breathe into the feeling for 60–90 seconds.
Let it move without analyzing it.
Most emotions peak and pass if you stop interrupting them.

4. Ask It

"What do you need right now?"

Sometimes it's rest. Sometimes it's to speak up. Sometimes it's to cry, move, laugh, or write.

Listen. Your body knows.

5. Shift It (Gently)

Once you've felt the feeling, you can choose to shift your state—not as avoidance, but as evolution.

Try movement, nature, music, hydration, or any practice that feels **nourishing**, not forced.

Turning Emotion Into Momentum

Now here's the alchemy part:

Once you've felt your emotion, ask:

"How can I use this energy to fuel my next aligned action?"

- Anger can fuel bold boundaries.
- Grief can fuel clarity and redefinition.
- Fear can fuel preparation and courage.
- Longing can fuel a commitment to change.

That's emotional calibration:

You don't suppress the emotion. You convert it.

You turn raw energy into intentional direction.

What About Emotional Triggers?

Triggers are sacred teachers. They reveal where you're still vibrating in the past.

Instead of judging your reaction, get curious:
- What old story is being activated here?
- What belief does this emotion want me to examine?
- What part of me still needs acknowledgment or safety?

You don't have to fix it all at once.

Just start responding, not reacting. That's frequency mastery.

Quick Practice: 3-Minute Energy Shift

Feeling stuck emotionally? Try this quick reset.

1. **Set a timer for 1 minute.** Name and feel your emotions fully.
2. **Set another timer for 1 minute.** Move: shake, dance, stretch—whatever helps move energy.
3. **Final minute:** Take one breath and ask, "What's one small thing I can do next?"

That's it. That's a vibrational pivot.

Not performance. Not perfection. Presence.

Feeling Isn't Failure

If you're feeling big emotions, it doesn't mean you're "off track."

It means you're alive, responsive, and powerful enough to process what most people avoid.

Emotion is the **engine** behind manifestation.

You just need to learn how to drive it.

Chapter 8: The Body Frequency Link

Here's a hard truth most "manifestation" guides won't tell you: You can't maintain a high frequency in a body that's exhausted,

inflamed, or constantly in survival mode.
You can't "mindset" your way around a nervous system that's shot.
You can't meditate your way past a body that's begging for nourishment, rest, and regulation.
Your body is not separate from your energy.
It is your energy.
You can repeat all the affirmations.
You can set all the intentions.
But if your body is depleted—running on caffeine, sugar, stress, and shallow breaths—
Then your manifestation engine is idling on empty.
This chapter is about getting real.
Not with shame. Not with guilt. Not with wellness-washed pressure.
But with love. Respect. And a no-BS understanding of your body as your **primary broadcast tower.**

Your Body Is Your Broadcast Tower

Your thoughts are the spark.
Your emotions are the fuel.
But your body? Your body is the **antenna.**
Every single cell in you vibrates.
Your nervous system? It emits waves.
Your breath? It pulses rhythm through your field.
Your digestion? It affects your mood, which affects your magnetism.
Your body is your transmitter. Your receiver.
It is how you signal to the universe what you're ready for.
Think of it like this:

- When your body is clear, grounded, oxygenated, nourished, and rested → your **signal is strong**. You become a clear channel.
- When your body is foggy, inflamed, stressed, dehydrated, or tense → your **signal gets scrambled**. Static, distortion, weak output.

So if you've been doing all the inner work but your reality still feels blocked?

Check your physical vessel.

That's often where the misalignment hides.

Let's dig into the three core pillars of physical frequency: **Fuel, Breath, and Movement.**

1. Fuel: What You Eat Affects What You Emit

You don't need to follow a rigid diet.

You don't need to go vegan, paleo, raw, keto, or moon-charged.

But you do need to stop treating food as an afterthought.

Or worse—an enemy.

Every bite you eat either helps your body broadcast your desires—or dulls the signal.

This isn't about "good" vs. "bad" food.

It's about **vibrational support.**

Low-Vibe Foods (when consumed chronically):
- Processed sugars and chemical additives
- Energy drinks or coffee with zero hydration
- Over-salted, low-nutrient fast food
- Alcohol used to numb or escape
- Food eaten during stress, distraction, or emotional collapse
- These choices create internal chaos:
- Inflammation
- Blood sugar crashes
- Brain fog
- Mood swings
- Nervous system burnout

And guess what?

Chaotic internal states = scattered external signals.

High-Vibe Foods:

- Unprocessed meals (colorful plants, clean proteins, healthy fats)
- Hydrating fruits and vegetables
- Foods eaten slowly, mindfully, and with gratitude
- Warm meals that nourish your gut and ground your energy

You don't need perfection.

You need **awareness**.

Ask yourself every time you eat:

"Is this supporting my energy—or stealing from it?"

You're not just eating for survival.

You're fueling a frequency.

2. Breath: The Frequency Accelerator You Forgot

Let's talk about the most underrated tool in your manifesting toolkit:

Your **breath**.

It's free.

It's immediate.

And it's your fastest access point to nervous system regulation—which controls how you feel, how you respond, and what you attract.

When you're stuck in shallow, upper-chest, rapid breathing?

Your body is in survival mode.

Fight-flight-freeze is activated.

Your system is chaotic.

Your intuition goes offline.

But when you slow your breath—on purpose—you flip the switch.

Calm breath = calm brain = calm field.

And from there? You become a **magnet**.

Try this: 2-Minute Coherence Breath.

1. Inhale gently for 4 seconds.
2. Exhale slowly for 6 seconds
3. Repeat for 2 full minutes

4.   As you breathe, focus on a feeling of gratitude, peace, or ease
This isn't just relaxing.
 This is **energetic alignment in real-time**.
Your brainwaves shift.
 Your heart rate stabilizes.
 Your energy field becomes coherent.
 And the universe? It responds to coherence.
3. Movement: Motion = Manifestation
Stuck thoughts?
 Stuck emotions?
 Stuck energy?
You can't think your way out.
 You have to **move it out**.
Your body is not a problem to be solved.
 It's a vessel to be activated.
Movement isn't about punishment.
 It's about circulation. Flow. Frequency expansion.
You don't need a gym membership.
 You don't need a six-pack.
 You need to **engage** your body so it can help you manifest.
Try any of these daily:
- 5-minute barefoot walk in fresh air
- Dance to one high-energy song like nobody's watching (because nobody is)
- Stretch your spine and open your chest (your heart center = magnetism)
- Shake your limbs for 30 seconds to release tension and reset your field
- Rebounding (jumping lightly in place) to wake up your lymphatic flow

Movement clears stagnation.
 It unlocks frozen emotional patterns.

It returns you to presence.

Because your body holds **memory**.

Fear, pain, unprocessed trauma—it lives in your fascia, your breath, your hips, your chest.

When you move, you release.

When you release, you receive.

Bonus Frequency Factors

Want to take your physical alignment to the next level? These aren't mandatory, but they magnify your energy:

- **Hydration**: You're mostly water. Water carries electrical signals. So drink like your frequency depends on it—because it does.
- **Sleep**: This is when your brain detoxes, your body repairs, and your field realigns. Manifestation from burnout is a dead end.
- **Touch**: Hug someone. Get a massage. Touch your heart. Skin contact = oxytocin = safety = expansion.
- **Environment**: Clear your physical space. Open windows. Burn sage or light a candle. Shift the external to support the internal.

These small, often-overlooked things can drastically clean up your signal.

And when your signal is clean, your path becomes clear.

Your Body Isn't In the Way—It Is the Way

Stop treating your body like a machine to drag around.

Stop resenting it for being tired or slow or messy.

Stop ignoring its cues.

Your body is not a delay in your manifestation.

It's the **delivery system**.

When your body is grounded, you trust yourself.

When it's nourished, you radiate safety.

When it's moving, you become magnetic.

Do you want to raise your frequency?

Don't just journal.

Don't just visualize.

Get in your body.

Feel it. Fuel it. Listen to it. Trust it.

This isn't about six-packs or green juice.

It's about honoring the **instrument** you've been given to play this life with.

Because your body already knows the way.

It remembers the aligned state.

It's always trying to lead you back to coherence.

The question is:

Are you willing to stop ignoring it?

PART 3: Manifestation Mechanics

Chapter 9: Vision, Clarity, and the Power of Specificity

The Universe doesn't do "kind of."
It doesn't respond to hesitation.
It doesn't decode maybes.
It doesn't interpret vagueness.
It responds to clarity.
Crystal clarity.
So if your vision is foggy—if your desires are half-formed, hesitant, or hedged with "ifs"—your results will reflect that. Not because the Universe is ignoring you, but because your signal isn't sharp enough to lock onto.
You can't shoot an arrow if you don't know where the target is.
You can't hit the mark if your aim keeps changing.
This chapter is your compass reset.
It's how you stop manifesting fog and start commanding focus.
Because vague intentions lead to vague outcomes.
And you didn't come here for kind-of.
You came here for real.
You came here for alignment.
You came here for results.
Let's get specific.

Most People Don't Know What They Want
Here's the wild thing:
Most people don't know what they want.
They only know what they don't want.

- "I don't want to be broke."
- "I don't want to feel stuck."
- "I don't want to date toxic people anymore."
- "I don't want to stay in this job forever."

Okay… but what do you want?

If you want more money—how much, exactly?
By when?
For what?
What does "more" even mean to you?
If you want a better job—doing what, exactly?
Remote or in-person?
Fast-paced or calm?
What kind of boss? What kind of impact?
If you want love—what kind of relationship?
What qualities do you want to give and receive?
What's the energy like when you're together?
If you can't answer these clearly,
You're not manifesting—you're reacting.
And the truth is:
A fuzzy goal is impossible to reach.
Because you'll never even know when you've arrived.
Clarity = Confidence = Power
When you finally get specific, three powerful things happen:
1. **Your brain gets a filter.**
It starts scanning your environment for cues, clues, opportunities, and evidence that match the image.
2. **Your energy sharpens.**
You stop leaking attention. You stop entertaining distractions. You begin radiating decisiveness.
3. **Your actions become targeted.**
You waste less time. You stop chasing random paths. You move in alignment with what matters.
Clarity ends confusion.
It turns daydreaming into direction.
And once your frequency sharpens, your outer world begins to reflect it.
Vision Audit: Let's Get Clear

Ready to clean the fog off the lens?
Choose ONE area to focus on:
Money; Love; Career; Health; Lifestyle
Now complete these prompts without overthinking:
- **I want to experience...**
- **I'll know it's happening when...**
- **It would feel like...**
- **It would allow me to...**
- Now dig into details:
- If it's money—how much per month? By when? What's it for?
- If it's love—how do you feel when you're with them? What's the dynamic like?
- If it's a lifestyle—what time do you wake up? What do your mornings look like? Where do you live?

Clarity is permission.
It's saying: "This is what I want."
It's not a demand. It's an energetic declaration.
And when you make it, your entire field starts to reorient.
The path ahead gets brighter. The distractions get quieter.

Specific ≠ Rigid
Quick reminder:
Being specific doesn't mean being attached.
There's a huge difference between **vision** and **control**.
Example:
"I want a cozy home near the ocean, full of light and calm, where I feel inspired to write and create every day..."
That's clear, powerful, emotionally resonant.
Now compare it to:
"It has to be exactly 1,700 square feet with beige walls and must be on this block or it doesn't count."
The first is a frequency.

The second is a demand.
The Universe loves details.
But it also loves flexibility.
Your job:

- Tune the vibe
- Paint the picture
- Speak the way
- The Universe's job:
- Work out the details
- Move the pieces
- Deliver the opportunities aligned with your highest timeline

The "Why" Factor: Clarity with Depth

Here's how to make your vision even more magnetic:
Give it meaning.
Want $10K a month? Why?
What does that unlock in your life?
What changes because of it?
Here's a high-frequency example:
"I want to earn $10K/month so I can work on my terms, give to causes I care about, travel freely, and never again have to choose between purpose and survival."
That's not a goal.
That's a mission.
The "why" fuels the vision with emotional voltage.
It turns a wish into a pulse.
A number into a frequency.
And when does the Universe feel that?
It doesn't just respond—it **partners**.

Visualization: Don't Just See It—Be It

Once your vision is clear and your why is strong, it's time to step into it.

Close your eyes.

Picture a single day in your future life—not a vague dream, but a real, textured scene.

- What time do you wake up?
- What's the first thing you see?
- Who's next to you—or not?
- What are you drinking? Wearing? Creating?
- What does your body feel like?
- What are you working on?
- What are you excited about?

Now breathe into it.

Let your nervous system memorize it.

Let your body feel the frequency before it happens.

Because this isn't fantasy.

It's vibrational rehearsal.

You are teaching your energy to match the future you're calling in.

And when your internal reality matches your desired outcome,

External alignment becomes inevitable.

Final Reminder: The Universe Matches Precision

When you keep saying vague things like:

- "I just want to feel better…"
- "I hope something changes…"
- "Maybe someday…"

The Universe shrugs.

It doesn't know what to do with that.

But when you say:

- "This is what I want."
- "This is what it looks like."
- "This is why it matters to me."
- "This is what I'm ready to receive."

The Universe says:

"Now we're talking."

Suddenly resources show up, ideas arrive, and conversations click.

You meet the right people, you make the right moves, but not because of luck. Because your signal is **finally clear**.

So if you've been foggy, indirect, or unsure?

Don't judge it. Just sharpen the picture. Turn up the clarity.

Own your desires out loud. Be bold about the what and grounded in the why. Precision is power.

Clarity is the first step to calling it in.

Chapter 10: The Aligned Action Method

Here's the hard truth that spiritual bypassers hate to hear:
You can't manifest from your couch.
You can't Netflix and hope.
You can't just think it, journal it, and vibe it—without ever lifting a finger.
Visualization is powerful.
Vision boards are fun.
Vibe is essential.
But without action?
You're not manifesting. You're marinating in wishful thinking.
This chapter is your crash course in **Aligned Action**:
The art of doing less—but doing it better.
The discipline of intentional momentum.
The practice of turning vibration into movement.
Because energy needs a channel.
And your aligned action is the signal that says, "I'm ready."
First, Let's Debunk a Myth
"If I'm in alignment, it should feel effortless."
Wrong.
Alignment doesn't mean easy.
Alignment means authentic.
And sometimes, authenticity feels edgy as hell.

- Aligned action might scare you.
- It might stretch you.
- It might go against what other people expect of you.

But here's the core distinction:
Aligned action feels activating—not depleting.
You might feel nervous—but also lit up.
You might feel uncertain—but also deeply true to yourself.
It might challenge your comfort zone—but it will never require you

to abandon your truth.

Alignment can be uncomfortable.

But it is never in conflict with your core.

If it requires self-betrayal, it's not alignment. It's fear in disguise.

The 3 Filters of Aligned Action

Before you take any step—especially one that feels "productive"—run it through these three filters:

1. Is this connected to my vision?

→ Is it truly moving me forward, or just making me feel busy?

2. Is this coming from belief—not fear?

→ Am I doing this from grounded confidence, or anxiety and panic?

3. Does this feel resonant in my body?

→ When I imagine doing this, do I feel expanded or constricted?

If it's a yes to all three: Go. Do the thing. Now.

Don't wait for signs. The alignment is the sign.

Action Is Frequency Made Visible

Let's break this down clearly:

- Thoughts are internal.
- Emotions are energetic.
- **Action is energetic materialization.**

Every time you take a step—from writing the email to changing the habit to hitting "send"—you are translating your frequency into form.

Your actions are your energy made tangible.

Still not sure what you're manifesting?

Look at your last 10 decisions.

Look at your habits.

That's your real signal.

The Universe doesn't respond to what you say.

It responds to what you signal through your consistent choices.

The Ladder Method: Big Vision, Small Steps

Manifestation becomes paralyzing when you try to leap from Step 1 to Step 100 in one go.

Instead, use the **Ladder Method**:

Connect to your big vision. Then find the next smallest, clearest step that honors it.

Example:

- **Vision**: Launch a soul-led business.
- **Next ladder step**: Write one offer. Book one conversation. Name the project. Create a freebie.

It might seem underwhelming—but it's not.

Because each small action does two powerful things:

1. **It breaks stagnation** and shifts your energy into movement.
2. **It builds self-trust.** You're proving to yourself: "I take my vision seriously."

Small steps don't mean small results.

They're how every big outcome begins.

Consistency compounds faster than you think.

When You're Not Sure What to Do

Confusion is not a stop sign.

It's an invitation to move.

Clarity often comes through movement—not before it.

When you're unsure, try this:

- Ask: "If I already had my manifestation, what would I be doing today?"
- Then do one thing that version of you would already be doing.
- That's aligned action. That's future-self embodiment. That's time to collapse.

You stop waiting for the conditions to change.

You start becoming the version of you who lives in that reality.

Aligned ≠ Always Comfortable

Let's be real:

- Quitting the job that's draining your soul? Aligned.

- Walking away from the relationship that keeps shrinking your light? Aligned.
- Saying "no" to what no longer resonates—even when it's "good on paper"? Aligned.

Is it always easy? Nope.

Is it always cozy? Not even close.

But it's **truth in motion**.

And truth carries force.

Alignment isn't about comfort—it's about coherence.

And coherence fuels quantum results.

Alignment Isn't One-and-Done

This is not a "one good week and everything's perfect" journey.

Manifestation is not a single ritual—it's an energetic lifestyle.

It's sustained alignment.

Ongoing choice.

Real-time recalibration.

Make it a practice to check in:

- "Is this still aligned with my vision?"
- "Am I acting from faith—or reacting from fear?"
- "Where am I hesitating to act because I don't want to feel discomfort?"

Don't use self-awareness as a weapon.

Use it as a compass.

You don't have to be perfect—you just have to course-correct faster.

The Universe Moves Through You

You're not waiting for signs.

You are the sign.

Your movement is the delivery vehicle for your manifestation.

The clearer your frequency, the more seamlessly the universe flows through you—not just to you.

You are the bridge.

The conduit between idea and outcome.

The link between energetic potential and physical reality.
Your thoughts are the blueprints.
Your feelings are the fuel.
But your actions are the architecture.
Every email, every call, every boundary, every decision—it builds your reality, brick by energetic brick.
So stop waiting for some cosmic green light.
Start being the one who moves.
Because when you act from alignment,
The Universe doesn't just catch up—it joins you at full speed.

Chapter 11: Micro-Manifests: The 24-Hour Rule

Manifestation isn't just about landing the big things—dream houses, soulmates, multi-figure months. Those take time. They require alignment, consistency, and steady energetic attunement. But while you're working toward the macro, you need something else to keep your engine running:

Proof.

You need evidence. Feedback. Confirmation that all this energy work isn't just happening in a vacuum. You need the universe to whisper back, "Yes, you're on the right path. Keep going."

That's where micro-manifestation comes in. It's not about the big win. It's about **training your frequency to expect results**—and to recognize them. Quickly.

Let's talk about the 24-hour Rule. Your new daily tool for building belief momentum, in real-time.

What Is a Micro-Manifest?

A micro-manifest is a small, specific desire you call in within 24 hours. Think of it as a "frequency rep"—low-pressure, high-impact. Examples:

- A compliment from a stranger
- A flash of inspiration
- A free coffee or small gift
- A message from someone unexpected
- A sudden moment of peace or clarity

Tiny? Yes. Random? Not at all.

Each one is a message to your subconscious: "My energy has influence. My vibration is a signal."

When you start seeing that, everything changes.

- Confidence builds.
- Clarity sharpens.
- Your nervous system stops resisting and starts

aligning.

Why 24 Hours?
Two big reasons:

1. Urgency collapses doubt. You don't have time to spiral or sabotage. You just ask, align, and live.

2. Fast feedback trains belief. The quicker your results, the faster you embed the pattern:

"I ask. I receive. This works."

This isn't about control. It's about calibration. You're not testing the universe. You're training yourself to recognize its response.

How to Use the 24-Hour Rule
Try this today. Seriously, today.

1. Choose a Small, Specific Desire Not a lottery win. Something simple but clear:

- "I see a yellow butterfly."
- "I get a message from someone I've been thinking about."
- "I receive an unexpected compliment."
- "I feel calm for 15 minutes straight."

2. Write It Down with a Time Stamp Lock it in. Make it specific. "I intend to receive a kind word or gesture by 6 pm tomorrow."

3. Feel It for 60 Seconds Close your eyes. Picture it happening. Imagine the smile. The warmth. The moment. Let your body respond.

4. Let It Go (But Stay Open) This is key. No grasping. No obsession. You're not begging. You're open.

Go live your day. Expect the knock on the door.

What If Nothing Happens?
First: Don't spiral.

This is practice. Not a test.

- Were you open or tense?

- Was the ask too heavy or vague?
- Did you allow space for a surprise?

Refine it. Lighten up. Try again.

When people stop gripping the process, they start seeing results.

The Compounding Effect

The more you micro-manifest:

- The more regulated your nervous system becomes.
- The more grounded your energy feels.
- The easier it is to trust your power.

Each one is a vibrational deposit. You're building frequency muscle. Your system goes from:

"Is this real?" To: "Of course, things flow to me."

Add This to Your Daily Practice

Here's how to make it stick:

Morning:

- Set a 24-hour intention.
- Write it down.
- **Evening:**
- Reflect: Did something land? Did something shift?

Celebrate any feedback, even if it looks different than expected.

You're not tracking to control. You're tracking to **calibrate**. Let small wins rewire your entire story.

Proof Fuels Power

You don't need to wait six months to believe you're a powerful creator. You can show yourself **today**.

- One clear desire.
- One felt emotion.
- One real result.

That's all it takes to begin:

"This works. I work. I'm not waiting. I'm creating."

Chapter 12: Quantum Timing

Let's start with the big question every manifesto asks sooner or later:
"Why isn't it happening yet?"
You've been doing the work. Raising your vibration. Acting in alignment. Visualizing like a champ. Doing your breathwork. Saying the affirmations. Clearing your chakras. Journaling your desires until your hand cramps. And still—crickets. Or, if you're lucky, tiny breadcrumbs.

Here's what you need to hear (and maybe hate a little at first):
It's not taking too long. You're just using the wrong clock.
Manifestation doesn't run on human time. It runs on quantum timing—the rhythm of resonance, alignment, and readiness.
Let's unpack what that means.

Linear Time vs. Quantum Time
In linear time, life follows a straight line: "Step 1. Then step 2. Then step 3."
But in quantum time, things don't unfold chronologically. They unfold energetically.
"When you are aligned with it, it becomes available."
That means things can come fast—or not at all—depending on your frequency match.
And here's the twist:
Your idea of "ready" and the universe's idea of "ready" are rarely the same.
You might want it now. But are you embodying it now? Are you acting, thinking, and vibrating like someone who already has it? Manifestation isn't about desire. It's about identity.
And the universe doesn't respond to the things you wish for. It responds to the person you're being.

Delay ≠ Denial
Think about baking a cake. You mix the ingredients. You preheat the oven. You wait. If you yank it out 15 minutes too early, it's ruined. The pause doesn't mean something's gone wrong. The pause means

something is **baking.**

Sometimes the pause is preparation. Sometimes it's energetic protection. Sometimes it's the universe rerouting you to something better.

So instead of asking:

"Why isn't it here yet?" Start asking: "What else is aligning behind the scenes so this can arrive with power and permanence?"

Three Reasons It Feels "Slow" (But Isn't)

1. Your Frequency is Still Updating

You might be bouncing between the old you and the future you. One foot in each reality. That's not failure—it's calibration.

2. The External Conditions Aren't in Place—Yet

That opportunity or person you're calling in? They're on their way too. It's not always about your alignment. Sometimes the universe is syncing multiple timelines at once.

3. Your Nervous System Isn't Ready to Receive It

If your body doesn't feel safe holding the desire, it will block it subconsciously. Manifestation isn't just mindset—it's somatic. You have to feel safe having what you want.

Patience Isn't Passive

Let's reframe patience.

True patience = **energetic discipline.**

It's not sitting on your hands hoping. It's:

- Staying in your frequency.
- Practicing what you preach.
- Living as if it's already done.
- Choosing trust over control.

Impatience sends the signal: "I don't trust this."

But when you relax into presence, you become magnetic. You stop chasing. You start receiving.

Collapse Time With Alignment

Here's the quantum cheat code:

The more aligned you are, the faster time collapses.

How do you collapse time?
- **Clarity collapses confusion.**
- **Action collapses waiting.**
- **Embodiment collapses separation.**

When you become the version of you who already has it, the universe speeds up to match you.

That's not wishful thinking. That's energetic coherence.

Practice: The "Already Here" Protocol

To move from waiting to receiving:
1. **Write your desire in the past tense.**
    a. "I'm so grateful I received the perfect offer."
    b. "I'm thrilled to have met someone who sees me."
    c. **Ask yourself:**
    d. "If this were already real, what would I stop stressing about today?"
    e. "What would I focus on instead?"
2. **Do that thing.** Live from that frequency. Move like it's already yours. Speak from that version of you.

That's how you collapse time.

It's On Time, Even If It's Invisible

You are not behind. You are not being punished. You are not forgotten.

What you want is either:
- **Already arriving** in ways you can't yet see, or
- **Training you to become** the version of you who can hold it.

Both are sacred. Both are manifestations.

You don't have to be perfect. You just have to stay in the room. Stay in the frequency. Stay in the becoming.

Because the universe always delivers. Just not on your clock. On its own—which is better, bigger, and wiser than you think.

PART 4: Reality Design

Chapter 13: The Morning Frequency Formula

You don't need a perfect life.
You need a powerful morning.
Why? Because your first 30 minutes after waking are prime energetic real estate.
Your subconscious is open. Your nervous system is resetting. Your energy is malleable.
This is where your daily frequency gets built—or broken.
If you wake up, grab your phone, scroll through fear and comparison, check your email, and feel dread, guess what you're doing?
You're downloading chaos.
You're choosing contraction.
You're handing the remote control of your vibration to someone else before your feet even touch the floor.
But if you start your morning with **intention, presence, and energetic alignment**, your entire day moves from reaction to creation.
You prime your field for magnetism—before the world starts shouting at you.
This isn't about morning routines as performance.
It's about building a daily **Frequency Launch Sequence** that aligns you with the timeline you want.
Let's build your Morning Frequency Formula.

Why Morning Matters (Even If You Hate Mornings)
No, you don't need to become the smug person who's up at 4:30 doing sun salutations on a cliff.
This isn't about hustle.
It's about **energetic ownership**.
The first 30–60 minutes after you wake up is your most suggestible, impressionable time.
Your brain is in theta and alpha states.

Your body is transitioning from stillness into motion.

Your vibration is still soft clay.

Whatever you imprint during this window becomes your baseline.

Momentum begins here.

And momentum is the unspoken force behind every manifestation.

If you skip the inner alignment and jump straight into reactivity, your day becomes a chain of responses.

But if you begin with presence, power, and clarity?

You become a channel. A magnet. A creator—not a reactor.

The universe rewards those who **lead their frequency**.

The 5 Elements of a High-Vibe Morning

This is a modular system. You can tailor it. Scale it up or down.

But try to hit each energetic layer: stillness, thought, emotion, movement, and intention.

1. Silence or Stillness (5–10 minutes)

Before thoughts rush in, pause.

This can be:

- Meditation
- Prayer
- Breath awareness
- Eyes-closed stillness

Why?

Because silence lets your soul speak before your mind takes over.

It slows your system, connects you to your body, and creates space for higher guidance.

Stillness is not emptiness.

It's receptive power.

2. Intentional Thought

Direct your mind—don't let the internet do it.

Plant your mental seeds:

- Ask: "What do I need to embody today?"
- Affirm: "I am rooted, ready, and radiant."

- Journal: "This is the kind of day I'm creating…"

You don't have to write a novel.

Even one sentence of aligned thinking is a ripple that becomes a wave.

Your mind is not your enemy.

It's your megaphone. Program it.

3. Emotional Tuning

Thoughts spark frequency.

Emotions anchor it.

So ask:

What do I want to feel today?

And then—generate that.

Tools:

- **Visualization:** Picture yourself already living the reality you desire. See it. Feel it.
- **Music:** One powerful song can rewire your whole nervous system.
- **Movement:** Dance it. Stretch into it. Shake off yesterday's static.

You don't wait for emotional alignment. You **create** it.

4. Body Activation

Energy flows where circulation goes.

Even just 3–5 minutes of movement can signal your nervous system: "We're alive. We're safe. Let's expand."

Try:

- Yoga
- Walking
- Rebounding
- Qigong
- Even just spinal stretches and shoulder rolls

Pair it with hydration.

Drink a full glass of water—bonus if you add lemon or minerals.
Water + breath + motion = frequency conductor.

5. Alignment Trigger (Anchor Ritual)

Close your practice with a **cue** that locks in your frequency.
Ideas:

- Light a candle and declare your intention aloud.
- Write one word on a sticky note: "Power," "Peace," and "Magnetism."
- Tap your heart and say: "Let's go."
- Pull a card, ring a bell, or wear a piece of jewelry with intention.

Why this matters: **Your body remembers rituals.**

Do the same one each morning and your system starts responding automatically with the,

"Oh—we're tuning in now."

The Mini Morning Formula (For Busy or Low-Energy Days)

No time? Feeling off? Try this 3-minute energetic reboot:

1. **Breathe:** One deep inhale. One long exhale.
2. **Speak:** Say one clear intention aloud.
 "Today I move with clarity and calm."
3. **Feel:** Generate one elevated emotion.
 Gratitude, pride, ease—whatever you can access.
4. **Move:** Shake, stretch, or walk to the sink for water.
5. **Smile:** Fake or real, it doesn't matter—your brain shifts anyway.

That's it.

Three minutes. Full reset.

No excuses are needed.

Consistency > Perfection

You don't need to be a morning routine influencer.

You just need to **show up for your frequency**.

Some mornings you'll feel magic.

Some mornings it'll be messy.

Do it anyway.

Because the act of showing up is the rewire.

It tells your subconscious:

"This is who I am now. Someone who chooses alignment."

Over time, you're not just doing a practice.

You're becoming a person with an identity rooted in energetic leadership.

Manifestation becomes less of a stretch—and more of a reflex.

Don't Just Wake Up. Turn On.

Stop waking up to other people's agendas.

Stop giving your frequency away before the day even starts.

Stop reacting to life—transmit first.

Own your state.

Command your vibe.

Lead your field.

And let the day rise to meet the energy you built on purpose.

Chapter 14: Vibration Killers

You've been doing the work.
You're getting clear. You're raising your vibe. You're showing up.
You've felt the spark, the synchronicities, the flow.
And then, out of nowhere...

- Your focus slips.
- Your confidence dips.
- Your frequency feels scrambled like someone jammed static into your signal.
- You feel... off.

What happened?
You've hit a vibration killer.
These aren't moral failings. They're not signs you're failing at manifesting.
 They're simply energetic sinkholes—subtle or sneaky forces that **pull your system out of coherence.**
But here's the power move:
When you can identify them, you can transmute them.
 Let's name the top vibration disruptors—and build tools to shift back into alignment fast.
Vibration Killer #1: Fear (Especially the Sneaky Kind)
Not all fear wears fangs.
 Some of it wears logic. Some of it wears your mother's voice. Some of it wears ambition dressed in anxiety.
It sounds like:

- "What if I get this and lose it?"
- "What if I'm not enough to sustain this?"
- "What will they think if I go for it?"
- "This is too good to be true..."

Fear doesn't always yell.

Sometimes it whispers from the shadows of your subconscious, casting doubt on your worth, your safety, or your timeline.
Here's the truth:

Fear isn't weakness. It's data.

It's your nervous system saying, "This is unfamiliar."

But unfamiliar doesn't mean wrong.

It means you're expanding.

Reframe the fear:

- Name it out loud: "This is fear speaking. Got it."
- Thank you for trying to protect you.
- Let it ride in the car—but don't let it drive.

Manifestation doesn't require fearlessness.

It requires awareness, courage, and forward movement anyway.

Vibration Killer #2: Overthinking

Let's call this what it is:

Mental clutter disguised as control.

Overthinking feels productive—but it's just procrastination with better PR.

When you spiral in thought:

- You disconnect from the body (where your true power lives)
- You scramble your intuitive signal
- You confuse possibility with probability

The universe doesn't respond to endless analysis.

It responds to coherence: thought, emotion, and action aligned.

Interrupt the loop:

- Ask: "Is this thought moving me toward my vision—or away from it?"
- Ground into your body. Place a hand on your chest or belly.
- Take one aligned action, even if it's tiny. Movement is

medicine.

Thought without embodiment is noise.

Thought with action is power.

Vibration Killer #3: Low-Energy People

This one's real. And sometimes hard.

It's not about cutting people out cold.

It's about recognizing: that **not every connection feeds your frequency.**

Some people:

- Operate from constant survival mode
- Live for drama cycles
- Don't believe change is possible—and resent that you do
- Can't celebrate your expansion because it threatens their stability

This doesn't make them villains.

But it **does** make them misaligned.

Energetic Boundaries 101:

- Notice how you feel after spending time with someone.
- Don't explain or defend your growth.
- Give less access to those who pull you into old identities.

You're not better than anyone.

But you are responsible for the quality of energy you consume and absorb.

When You Can't Avoid the Drain

Let's be honest:

You can't always avoid the stressor, the person, the trigger.

Sometimes it's a boss, a roommate, a parent, or your brain on autopilot.

But you can still **claim your energy sovereignty.**

Try this **Frequency Bubble Technique (1 Minute)**:
1. Close your eyes and take 3 deep breaths.
2. Visualize a sphere of shimmering light surrounding your body. Any color that feels powerful.
3. Say (aloud or in your mind):
"This is my energetic field.
I am centered. I am clear. I am grounded in my truth."
Repeat when needed. Before meetings, after phone calls, and before walking into triggering spaces.
This isn't just imagination.
This is frequency reinforcement.

Bonus Killers (That Sneak In Daily)
Let's name a few more subtle disruptors that creep in:
- **Comparison:** Your power can't live in someone else's timeline.
- **Toxic media scrolls:** Your subconscious digests everything. Feed it accordingly.
- **Internalized scarcity loops:** "There's not enough time/money/love/space…" kills flow.
- **Over-identification with your past:** You are not your old story. That was a version. You're evolving.

Quick rescue:
- Go outside. Touch a tree. Seriously.
- Move your body for 2 minutes.
- Speak a new truth out loud: "I'm safe to expand. I'm safe to receive."

Vibe ≠ Isolation
You don't need to become a hermit to protect your field.
This isn't about hiding—it's about **selective exposure**.
Curate your life like you curate your playlist:

- Spend more time with **expanders**—people who normalize growth, creativity, and belief.
- Unfollow accounts that drain, shame, or trigger your nervous system.
- Say "no" when your energy says "not today."

Your tribe reflects your vibration.

Choose wisely—and let it evolve.

Protect Your Signal Like It's Sacred (Because It Is)

You wouldn't leave your bank account open for anyone to access.

You wouldn't let random strangers walk into your house uninvited.

So why let just anything walk into your frequency?

Set boundaries.

Catch the static.

Declutter the mind.

Pause when fear whispers.

Choose presence over performance.

Trust yourself to reset, realign, and rise again.

Your energy is your currency.

Guard it. Nourish it. Amplify it.

And let the world meet you at your clearest, most aligned signal.

Chapter 15: Using Environment as an Energetic Amplifier

Your environment is always speaking.
To your mind. To your body. To your energy.
And here's the truth that most people overlook:
Your environment is either **fueling your frequency**
—or it's slowly, silently, and consistently **draining it.**
There is no such thing as neutral space.
Everything around you—sights, sounds, smells, textures, digital noise—is either amplifying your alignment or distorting your signal.
So if you're doing the inner work—visualizing, affirming, meditating, manifesting—and you still feel stuck, scattered, or off-track…
Look around.
Is your outer world reinforcing your vision?
Or is it reinforcing your old patterns?
This chapter is about **environmental alignment.**
Not just making things "look nice."
But turning the spaces you live in—physical, digital, energetic—into
a match for your highest self.
Let's turn your life into a frequency amplifier.

Your Environment Is a Mirror
Every space tells a story.
Your room. Your phone. Your desk. Your car.
They all speak to your subconscious.
And your subconscious speaks to the universe.

- If your bedroom is chaotic, your nervous system is on edge—even while you sleep.
- If your workspace is cluttered, your mind mimics the noise.
- If your phone is filled with drama, distractions, and doomscrolling, guess what your energy field absorbs?
- None of this is "just stuff."

It's frequency. Input. Signal.
- Ask yourself:
- "If someone walked into this space, what story would it tell about who I am becoming?"
- "Does this environment reflect where I've been—or where I'm going?"
- When you shift your outer space to match your future self, you start magnetizing that future faster.

The Three Environments That Shape Your Vibration

1. Physical Space (Your 3D World)

Your home. Your car. Your kitchen. Your closet. Your desk.
This is the most obvious—but often most neglected—frequency field.

Because your body is always in communication with your surroundings.

Audit Questions:
- Is this space calming or chaotic?
- Do I feel lighter or heavier after spending time here?
- Would my future self feel supported here—or distracted?
- **Shift Strategies:**
- Clear one surface per day.
- Add an object that holds meaning (photo, quote, crystal, token).
- Let go of one thing that feels like an old version of you.

This isn't about aesthetic perfection.

It's about energetic permission.

Clarity in your space = clarity in your signal.

2. Digital Space (Your Invisible Home)

Your phone is your second nervous system.

Your laptop is your co-creator.

Your online world is an ecosystem that's either nourishing or numbing you.

Audit Questions:
- What's the first thing I see when I open my phone?
- Who and what am I unconsciously giving attention to every day?
- What apps or accounts raise my energy—and which drop it?
- **Shift Strategies:**
- Change your wallpaper to your vision board, a mantra, or a power word.
- Unfollow 10 accounts that no longer reflect your values.
- Create "frequency folders"—collections of bookmarks, videos, images, or songs that restore alignment instantly.

Your digital hygiene is part of your spiritual hygiene.

Clean it like your life depends on it—because energetically, it does.

3. Energetic Space (The Felt Field)

This is the intangible but powerful layer:

The vibe of a room, a routine, or even your schedule.

Ever walked into a room and felt tension before anyone said a word?

That's energetic residue.

Audit Questions:
- Do I feel safe, expansive, and present in this space?
- Is there stagnant energy that needs to be moved or cleared?
- Am I honoring my space as sacred—or rushing through it unconsciously?

Shift Strategies:

- Open windows. Let fresh air and sunlight reset the field.
- Light a candle, incense, or diffuse oils with intention.
- Play sound frequencies, mantra music, or binaural beats.
- Use touchstones: a meaningful object, a scent, a sound that grounds you instantly.

You don't need to save everything or buy fancy tools.

You just need intention + attention.

Create Anchor Points in Your Space

Anchor points = physical cues that reconnect you to your frequency. They're tiny. But powerful.

Why? Because repetition rewires identity—and anchors remind you of who you're becoming.

Examples:
- A post-it with your future identity written in bold: "I am a calm, powerful, magnetic creator."
- A coin or charm you touch before every call or creative session.
- A framed vision statement or dream destination on your wall.
- A piece of clothing that represents the energy of your next level.

Tip: Place them where you habitually look—mirrors, doors, notebooks, lock screens.

Every glance becomes a micro-moment of alignment.

Redesign Without Overwhelm

You don't need to burn everything down and start over.

Manifestation isn't about extremes. It's about calibration.

Start here:
- Clear one drawer that annoys you.
- Make your bed with intention.

- Add one soft lamp to your workspace.
- Remove one object that no longer fits the vibe.

Ask:

"Does this item belong in my future life?"

"Does this layout help me breathe deeper, think clearer, and create easier?"

Your outer world is a vision board. Make it reflect the energy you want to live inside.

Your Space Doesn't Have to Be Fancy—Just Intentional

Forget Pinterest. Forget influencers.

Your environment isn't about impressing people.

It's about **informing your frequency.**

- Want peace? Prioritize simplicity, softness, and quiet.
- Want abundance? Remove anything that screams "scarcity" or "settling."
- Want creativity? Surround yourself with art, color, music, and light.

The goal isn't perfection. It's **congruence.** You want to walk into your space and feel:

"Yes. This matches me."

Your Space Is Not Separate—It's Strategic

Manifestation doesn't live in your vision board.

It lives in your **moment-by-moment environment.**

You may not control the whole world.

But you can control what's on your nightstand.

What's on your screen?

What's on your walls?

What you wake up into.

So take the time to ask:

"Is my environment an amplifier of my energy—or an anchor to my past?"

Because when your **space echoes your vision**,
 when your **surroundings reflect your becoming**,
 When your **field is clean, curated, and intentional**…
That's when the universe shows up and says:
"You're ready. Let's build it here."

Chapter 16: Money, Love & Career

Let's get real.
You didn't come here for fluff.
You didn't pick up this book just to collect quotes or light candles and hope something happens.
You're here because you want to **see it.**
In your bank account.
In your relationships.
In your career.
In your reality.
You want the shift—the measurable, tangible, undeniable kind.
And not just one-time magic. You want a way of life that supports sustainable transformation.
This chapter isn't about theory.
It's about **integration.**
We're diving into how to **manifest real-world results** in three key life arenas:

- Money (Abundance & Flow)
- Love (Connection & Worth)
- Career (Purpose & Power)

The principles stay the same:
Clarity. Frequency. Alignment. Action.
But now, we're filtering them through intention-driven focus to help you move the needle where it matters most.

Manifesting Money: From Scarcity to Sovereign Flow
Let's strip the noise:
Money is energy.
It is not moral.
It does not judge.
It simply flows toward coherence—toward people who feel safe receiving, holding, and directing it.

If you've been stuck in scarcity—feeling blocked, anxious, or disempowered when it comes to money—don't shame yourself. Recognize that you've been broadcasting from an old signal. And now it's time to **update the frequency.**

Common Money Blocks:
- Obsessing over what's missing, rather than what's possible
- Believing it's "wrong" to ask, charge, or receive
- Waiting for permission or proof before taking bold steps
- Internalizing beliefs like "I'm not good with money" or "Rich = selfish"
- **Frequency Shifts That Attract Abundance:**
- Set a specific intention (ex: "$3,000/month to support my writing and travel")
- Practice feeling **safe with money**—even imaginary money
- Align your spending/giving with trust, not guilt
- Take brave action **before** the proof arrives
- Rewire your beliefs: "I get to thrive. My receiving helps others."

Practices:
- **Journal Prompt:**

"If I fully trusted money would flow, I would stop ___ and start ___."
- **Micro-Manifest:**

"I call in $25 or a sign of unexpected abundance in the next 24 hours."
- **Embodiment Step:**

Dress, walk, or speak as the version of you who earns with ease.

When you **move differently**, money starts moving too.

Money doesn't respond to begging—it responds to **boldness and belief.**

Manifesting Love: From Lack to Magnetic Alignment

Love doesn't come when you "fix yourself."

It comes when you finally realize:

"I am already the one I've been waiting for."

Manifesting love isn't about finding the perfect partner.

It's about embodying the version of you who no longer **settles**, **chases**, or **shrinks** for love.

You attract what mirrors your emotional baseline.

Not just what you want—but what you believe you're worthy of.

Common Love Blocks:

- Needing someone to complete or rescue you
- Holding onto past pain or mistrust
- Being vague in your desires
- Choosing "almost enough" over being alone
- **Love-Frequency Alignment:**
- Define your emotional standard: "In my ideal relationship, I feel seen, cherished, respected…"
- Embody that feeling now—through rituals, words, choices
- Say no to anything that's misaligned—even if it's "almost right"
- Create actual space: clear the clutter, the apps, the exes, the fear

Practices:

- **Visioning Prompt:**

"In my aligned relationship, I feel…" (go deep—safety, passion, playfulness, support)

- **Self-Love Mirror Ritual:**

Look yourself in the eyes and affirm: "I am the love I seek."

- **Space Clearing:**

Let go of one thing—physical or emotional—that blocks energetic room for love to land.

You don't attract healthy love by trying harder.

You attract it by becoming unavailable for anything less than alignment.

Manifesting Career: From Struggle to Aligned Success

Let's be honest:

Your work shouldn't crush your soul.

You're not here to grind through a job that drains you or shrink to fit roles that aren't made for you.

Whether you're ready to launch a business, shift careers, get promoted, or just feel alive in your work—this is your moment to stop playing small.

Common Career Blocks:

- Staying stuck in "safe" work while your passion withers
- Thinking you're "not qualified yet" or "too late"
- Dimmed ambition to avoid judgment or rejection
- Waiting for external permission instead of **choosing yourself**
- **Frequency Shifts That Unlock Career Flow:**
- Get radically clear: What lights you up? What impact do you want to have?
- Own your current skills—and trust you'll build the rest
- Take aligned, messy action instead of over-preparing forever
- Act as if your dream job already chose you
- **Practices:**

- **Ideal Workday Vision:**

"I wake up feeling __. I spend my time doing __. I work with people who __."

- **Micro-Move:**

Update your resume. DM a mentor. Pitch your idea. Claim your LinkedIn headline.

- **Embodiment:**

Dress for the job you're calling in. Speak about your work with power and clarity.

Your career doesn't evolve because you wait.

It evolves because you move—intentionally, energetically, and courageously.

One Area at a Time, Full Focus

Manifestation works best when you channel your energy like a laser—not a flashlight.

Pick one area:

Money

Love

Career

And run it through this clarity protocol:

1. **What do I want—specifically?**
2. **How will I know it's happening? (feeling, action, sign)**
3. **What belief do I need to hold as truth?**
4. **What one action can I take this week from that belief?**

Write it. Speak it. Feel it. Act from it.

Then track:

- What shifts internally?
- What signs or synchronicities appear?
- What small wins start flowing?

Because the goal isn't just the outcome.

It's becoming the version of you who creates outcomes on command.

That's the real power.

That's when manifestation becomes your method—not just your hope.

PART 5: Beyond the Wish List

Chapter 17: When the Universe Says "Not Yet"

You've been aligning. You've been acting.
You've been believing. You're in it.
Doing the work. Living the frequency.
Showing up with clarity, courage, with consistency.
And still—
Nothing.
Or worse:
The job interview ghosted you. The perfect apartment slipped away.
The promising date disappeared. The launch didn't land.
The money didn't move. The clarity turned to fog.
And your brain screams:
"What else do I have to DO?"
Pause. Right here.
Take a breath.
Because **this** moment—the stall, the silence, the ache—is the moment that defines most people's journey.
It's the place where many quit.
Where they collapse into doubt, self-blame, or despair.
But it's also where the most powerful manifestos do something else entirely:
They lean in.
The Truth About "Not Yet"
What if that silence isn't punishment… but precision?
What if the delay is **data**?
What if "not yet" is sacred?
What if this moment is building capacity, not breaking you down?
"Not yet" doesn't mean "no."
It means:
"Not like this."
"Not with that."

"Not until you're ready to receive the version that lasts."
The universe isn't just trying to give you what you asked for.
It's trying to align you with what you're capable of holding.
And sometimes that requires rewiring—of belief, of identity, of environment, of emotional bandwidth.

Why Delays Are Part of the Plan
Let's be clear:
- You are **not** being punished.
- You are **not** failing.
- You are **not** invisible.

You are being refined.
The universe sees 10,000 angles you can't.
It sees behind the curtain.
It knows the contracts you've forgotten.
It's rearranging, recalibrating, and timing you for your highest outcome—not your fastest one.
And sometimes the thing you're clinging to isn't the thing you're aligned with.
It's just what looks familiar, close, or easy.

3 Reasons You Might Be Hearing "Not Yet"
1. You're Close—But Still Gripping
You've done the energetic alignment.
But part of you still needs the result to feel "safe," "valid," or "worthy."
That's not a moral failure. That's just attachment energy.
And attachment blocks flow.
Try this instead:
"I desire this—but I am whole either way."
That's liberation. That's magnetism.

2. You're Ready—But the Infrastructure Isn't
The opportunity, the partner, the platform—it might still be forming.

The missing piece may not even be about you.

Your timeline isn't slow. It's being synchronized with a larger architecture.

You're not being left behind. You're being timed.

3. You're Being Diverted Toward Something Higher

What you thought was the thing might just be a stepping stone.

Sometimes the "failure" is the redirection that protects you from smallness, mediocrity, or misalignment.

What if the "no" is a cosmic reroute?

Not away from your dream—but toward the version that honors you?

What to Do in the Waiting

This is the initiation.

This is the forge.

This is where your real power is tempered.

It's easy to stay aligned when everything's flowing.

But the magic happens when you stay aligned even when it isn't.

Try this 3-part recalibration ritual:

1. Re-Center Daily

Ask:

"Who am I becoming—regardless of outcomes?"

Reconnect to your core identity: the one who trusts, who creates, who keeps showing up.

Let the results go.

Lock into your self-concept.

2. Move Anyway

Keep acting from belief.

Send the email. Take the walk. Share the post. Write the thing.

Your consistency is not for the outcome—it's for the alignment.

"I believe it's already mine, so I act like it."

3. Shift the Question

Stop asking:

"Why isn't it here yet?"

Start asking:

"What's next?"

This keeps you in forward motion. It keeps your energy fresh.

It stops the loop of self-blame and plants you back in power.

What to Do When It Hurts

Let's not bypass this:

"Not yet" can feel like heartbreak.

You thought it was it.

The person. The offer. The miracle.

And now it's gone—or worse, suspended in silence.

Don't rush to fix it.

Don't spiritualize the ache away.

Let it hurt. Let it be real.

Cry. Rage. Journal.

But don't make the pain your **meaning.**

Don't make the moment your identity.

You are not broken.

You are being shaped.

Your dream didn't vanish.

It just found a better doorway.

Quick Practice: Energetic Recovery Ritual

When you're in the fog—try this:

1. **Close your eyes.**
2. **Breathe in:**

    "I trust the timing of my life."

3. **Breathe out:**

    "I release attachment to how and when."

4. **Visualize your dream** behind a curtain.

    Not gone. Just hidden. Still real. Still coming.

5. **Ask:**

    "What's one small thing I can do today to honor my

power?"

Do that thing.

Then stop trying to control the rest.

It's Yours—If You Stay Available to It

The path will change.

The packaging will surprise you.

The timing may test you.

But the frequency never lies.

And the universe never wastes aligned energy.

If you keep showing up—with open hands, honest intention, and grounded power—what's meant for you **can't miss you.**

It may take longer than you wanted.

But it won't take longer than it needs to.

So:

- Breathe.
- Soften.
- Trust.
- And hold your frequency like it already belongs to you.

Because it does.

Even now.

Especially now.

Would you like this version added to your manuscript as a chapter?

Chapter 18: Signs, Synchronicities & How to Read the Field

Ever think about someone and then they text you? See the same number repeatedly? Hear a song that perfectly answers the question in your head. Dream about something, then see a billboard or a headline that echoes the same theme? Those aren't coincidences. They're communications. The universe is whispering. Sometimes shouting. Sometimes slipping secret notes into your experience.
The universe doesn't speak English. It speaks about energy, pattern, emotion, and timing. It speaks through signs, nudges, echoes, and synchronicities. And when your frequency is aligned—when you're grounded, aware, and open—the field around you starts responding in real time. You'll start to notice that everything is alive with meaning. That everything is mirroring something in you.
But if you're not paying attention? You miss the memo. You scroll past the message. This chapter is about learning how to tune in. To read the field. Stop asking, "Is that a sign?" and start trusting: "I hear you."

What Is a "Sign"?
A sign is a personal symbol that carries energetic meaning. It's not about superstition—it's about soul-level pattern recognition. It's a code. A message. A flash of resonance.
The universe is always responding to you. Always. Signs are how it says:

- "Yes—keep going."
- "That's not for you."
- "Time to shift."
- "You're in sync."
- "You're thinking it—so here's your confirmation."

You don't need to force signs. You don't need to demand proof. You just need to be aware. Awake. Receptive. When you're attuned, the messages become unmistakable.

What Is a Synchronicity?
A synchronicity is a meaningful coincidence that arrives with perfect timing. It's when the outer world lines up so precisely with your inner world that you can't write it off as random.

Examples:
- Meeting the exact person you just journaled about
- Seeing your dream city everywhere after saying you wanted to move
- Hearing your next step spoken aloud by a stranger
- Finding the exact quote you needed to hear, three times in one day
- Seeing 11:11 just as you set a bold intention

Synchronicity is not "woo." It's not magical thinking. It's a function of resonance. When your frequency aligns with a potential, the field around you begins to organize events, people, and patterns to reflect that to you.

Synchronicity is confirmation from the universe: "Yes. You're tuned in. Keep following this thread."

How to Start Seeing More Signs
You don't attract more signs by begging for them. You attract them by calibrating your attention.

Step 1: Set a Clear Ask
Every morning or whenever you need guidance, try this:

"Universe, show me a clear sign that I'm on the right path. Make it obvious. Make it feel like a YES. I'm listening."

Then release it. Let it go. Go live your life. The sign will show up—but only if you're not obsessing over it.

Step 2: Choose a Symbol (Optional)
Sometimes a symbol helps create trust and recognition. You might say:

"If I see a yellow butterfly, I'll take that as confirmation." "If this person calls me today, I'll know it's alignment." "If I hear this lyric again, I'll trust it's time to act."

The symbol doesn't matter. What matters is the **feeling** it gives you. The resonance it activates. Your subconscious will start scanning the field to match your energetic request.

Step 3: Tune In to Your Body

Signs are often felt more than seen. The best confirmations land in your nervous system first. You might feel:

- Goosebumps
- A softening or expansion in your chest
- A full-body YES
- Instant calm or emotional clarity

The external sign is only part of it. The internal reaction tells you if it's real.

Common Signs & What They Might Mean

Use this as inspiration—not dogma. You assign the meaning. Your energy gives it context.

Sign	Possible Meaning
Repeating numbers	You're in alignment. Pay attention to your thoughts.
Animals/insects	Embodied symbolism—e.g., butterfly = transformation
Songs/lyrics	Subconscious message or emotional guidance

Unexpected delays	Course correction. Redirection. Not punishment.
Everything flows easily	Full resonance. Alignment. Green light. Go all in.

Ultimately, a sign is only as powerful as the meaning you give it.

Red Light vs. Green Light

Want to know if something is for you? Watch how it moves.

When something is aligned:
- Doors open effortlessly
- People respond quickly and with enthusiasm
- You feel calm, safe, grounded—even if it's big or new
- You're pulled forward by desire, not pushed by pressure

When something is not aligned:
- Roadblocks keep stacking up (not challenges—misalignment)
- Your energy drops, your mind scrambles, your body contracts
- You keep trying to "force" momentum
- It feels like an uphill battle with no payoff

Learn to tell the difference between resistance that's **growth-based** and resistance that's **misalignment-based.**

What If You Don't See Any Signs?

You're never actually signless. You might just be:
- Too distracted
- Too noisy
- Too stressed
- Too fixated on one outcome

To clear the channel:
- Spend 10 minutes in nature or silence
- Turn off notifications
- Skip social media for a day
- Journal whatever "random" things keep coming up
- Before bed, ask: "Send me a sign tomorrow—and help me recognize it."

The universe doesn't yell. It responds to quiet minds and curious hearts.

Final Practice: The Daily Field Check-In

Start every day with 3 simple questions:
1. What energy am I putting out today?
2. What am I ready to receive?
3. How will I know if I'm being guided?

Write it down. Revisit it at night. Over time, you'll see patterns. You'll strengthen your intuition. And you'll realize how often the universe speaks when you listen.

The Universe Is Speaking—Are You Available?

You're not asking for magic. You're asking for mirroring. The universe reflects your state to you through:
- Images
- Numbers
- People
- Songs
- Delays
- Symbols
- Serendipities

When you stop looking for signs of fear—and start opening to them from trust—you become fluent in a language most people never learn.

It's not about superstition. It's about presence. It's about relationships. It's about co-creation.

Once you learn how to read the field, you'll never again wonder, "Am I being supported?" You'll know. You'll feel it. Because you'll see it everywhere.

Chapter 19: Vibrational Leadership

There comes a moment on the manifestation path when the focus starts to shift. You've seen the tools work. You've felt the alignment. You've called things in—maybe not perfectly, but powerfully. You've manifested small wins. You've had moments of awe. You've seen yourself co-create in ways you can't quite explain.

And then you realize: "It's not just about what I can get... it's about who I can become."

That's the turning point. That's the moment you step into Vibrational Leadership. Not the kind that posts inspirational quotes all day. Not the kind that wears fake smiles and filters. Not the kind that talks louder to be heard.

But the kind that holds such clear, grounded, magnetic energy that the room recalibrates when you walk in.

The kind of presence that doesn't need attention—because it already has an impact.

This chapter is about becoming a living, breathing frequency that others feel—without needing to prove, push, or perform.

What Is Vibrational Leadership?

It's not about status or title. It's not about having more followers or being the loudest voice in the room. It's about authentic resonance. You don't lead with your words. You lead with your alignment.

You become:

- The calm in the chaos
- The mirror of what's possible
- The anchor when everything else is spinning
- The energetic permission slip for others to rise

People don't remember what you said. They remember how they felt in your presence. Your energy gives them access to their own.

You become a portal—not because you try, but because you are tuned in.

Why This Matters for Manifestation
When you step into vibrational leadership, manifestation changes shape. The more you embody your frequency:
- The faster people, resources, and support show up
- The more aligned opportunities seem to "find you"
- The less you hustle, chase, or overthink

Because you're no longer trying to manifest. You've become the energy that manifests.

You're not broadcasting want—you're radiating embodiment. That's not magic. That's energetic maturity. That's coherence in action.

You shift from: "I hope it works" to "I trust who I am."

And that's when the field starts moving mountains on your behalf.

The 3 Pillars of Vibrational Leadership

1. Self-Integrity

You do what you say you'll do—even when no one is watching. You clean up your energy before projecting it onto others. You stay in alignment with your values, not for approval—but for coherence.

The most powerful people don't control others. They master themselves. They walk in truth. They live what they teach.

Self-integrity builds trust—not just with others, but with the field.

2. Emotional Transparency

You don't fake it. You feel it. You show others what it means to move through fear with courage—not to hide it under fake confidence.

You model the beauty of being real. You don't pretend to be perfect. You permit people to feel without shame.

Vulnerability is a high frequency. It builds intimacy, trust, and energetic connection faster than performance ever could.

3. Energetic Generosity

You lead from overflow—not obligation. You give because you're grounded—not because you're trying to get something in return. You amplify others without shrinking yourself. You hold space without losing your center.

You remind people of who they are—not through fixing, but through being. That's the art of true leadership: impact without imposition.

Who You Are Is the Strategy
You don't need the perfect pitch, brand aesthetic, or elevator speech. You need coherence. When your words, actions, energy, and intention are aligned—you become the strategy.
Whether you're:
- Building a business
- Parenting with presence
- Holding space for clients or friends
- Leading a community or team
- Healing in private
- Showing up in your daily life with presence and clarity

Your energy leads first. And people feel it. And more importantly, they trust it.

Alignment becomes your calling card. Authenticity becomes your magnet. Your field becomes your invitation.

The Magnetic Mirror Practice
At the start of your day, try this:
Ask: "Who am I becoming today—just by how I show up?"
Choose one frequency to lead with:
- Calm
- Clarity
- Groundedness
- Joy
- Boldness
- Trust
- Lightness

Then set an intention:

"Let this energy move through me today. Let it touch the people I meet. Let it shape how I respond to the world."

Don't try to perform it. Don't try to force it. Let it radiate.

You'll notice:

- People respond differently
- Conversations deepen
- Synchronicities increase
- You feel anchored, even in uncertainty

Legacy Isn't What You Leave Behind—It's What You Carry Into Every Room

You are a walking field of vibration. You are always leading—whether you realize it or not. You can:

- Make people feel safe just by being grounded
- Inspire them just by being real
- Elevate the energy of a space without saying a word

That's leadership. That's presence. That's manifestation at the highest level.

Manifestation is not just about what you have. It's about who you **become** in the process.

And when you become magnetic—authentically, consistently, and generously—everything else rearranges to meet you there.

Because the field always responds to truth. Because energy never lies. Because who you are… is already enough.

Your final formula for infinite becoming

You've made it. You've learned what manifestation is—not wishful thinking, but energetic alignment plus conscious action. You've tuned your frequency, rewired your stories, raised your standards, faced your doubt, and moved anyway. You've stopped begging the universe to save you and started becoming the version of you who co-creates with it. You've noticed the signs, followed the nudges, reclaimed your power, and started anchoring into identity—not just the outcome. You've shifted from force to flow, from fear to faith. Now, you don't just know how to manifest. You are the manifesto.

But here's the real secret: Manifestation isn't a destination. It's an identity. It's not something you "do" once. It's who you wake up as. Who you return to when you forget. Who you claim again and again—no matter what the world looks like. It's in your breath, your walk, your gaze, your silence, your standards. It's not about the vision board anymore. It's about the embodied vision.

This final chapter is your creed. Your contract. Your compass. Not something to memorize. Something to live. To anchor. To echo. Let's close this book—and open your next chapter.

The Manifestor's Creed
I am the source of my frequency. I am the one I've been waiting for. I do not wait for the world to permit me. I give it to myself. I decide who I am, how I show up, and what I call in.
I know that energy is a language. And I speak it fluently—through my thoughts, feelings, actions, and presence. Every moment, I send a signal. And the universe responds in kind.
I trust that what is meant for me cannot be missed. Delays do not break me. Detours do not derail me. I meet each moment with presence, not panic—because I know alignment always finds its way. Even in uncertainty, I anchor into truth. Even in doubt, I walk in devotion.
I no longer chase. I choose. I do not hustle for worthiness. I move from wholeness. I am not here to beg. I am here to resonate. I am the match for what I desire.
I align. I act. I receive. And I repeat—with clarity, courage, and faith.
I do not fake positivity. I feel powerful. I allow my emotions. I move through my shadows. I own every part of me—not just the shiny ones. Because wholeness is my true vibration. My depth is part of my light.
I do not manifest alone. I am in dialogue with a universe that listens. I follow the signs. I respect the pauses. I celebrate the synchronicities. I honor the unseen. I know that invisible forces respond when I do my part.
I raise my standards and protect my energy. I am unavailable for chaos, confusion, and crumbs. I lead with clarity. I surround myself with resonance. I create space for miracles by removing what no longer aligns.
I live from the future I am creating—not the past I'm escaping. Every decision I make reflects the version of me I'm becoming. Every word, every breath, every choice is a vote for that future. Every breath is a signal: I am ready.

I am not waiting for the life I want—I am walking it. Right now. Right here. With intention. With devotion. With fire. I embody it before I see it. I believe it before I touch it.

I am the frequency. I am the magnet. I am the message. I am the channel. I am the manifester.

And I will become again, and again, and again— because that's what I came here to do. To create. To remember. To rise. To return to the truth.

This Isn't the End. It's the Embodiment.
You don't need more time. You don't need more proof. You don't need more "how."
You have everything you need. Right now. The question is no longer: "Can I do this?" The question is: "Will I become the version of me who does?"
You've got the tools. You've got the truth. You've got the spark. You've practiced the pause. You've followed the pull. You've watched the field respond.
Now take that frequency and go build the life that matches it. Go speak the language of your soul fluently. To be the lighthouse—not the lifeboat. Because the universe is already listening. And it's waiting for your signal.
So go send it. Go walk it. Go live it. And let the world rearrange in response.

www.ingramcontent.com/pod-product-compliance
Lightning Source LLC
Chambersburg PA
CBHW072200160426
43197CB00012B/2460